Joseph Bird

Protection Against Fire

and the best means of putting out fires in cities, towns and villages, with practical

suggestions for the security of life and property

Joseph Bird

Protection Against Fire
and the best means of putting out fires in cities, towns and villages, with practical
suggestions for the security of life and property

ISBN/EAN: 9783337256210

Printed in Europe, USA, Canada, Australia, Japan

Cover: Foto ©Andreas Hilbeck / pixelio.de

More available books at **www.hansebooks.com**

PROTECTION AGAINST FIRE,

AND

THE BEST MEANS OF PUTTING OUT FIRES IN CITIES, TOWNS, AND VILLAGES,

WITH

PRACTICAL SUGGESTIONS FOR THE SECURITY OF LIFE AND PROPERTY.

BY

JOSEPH BIRD.

An ounce of prevention is better than a pound of cure.

NEW YORK:

PUBLISHED BY HURD AND HOUGHTON.

Cambridge: The Riverside Press.

1873.

RIVERSIDE, CAMBRIDGE:
STEREOTYPED AND PRINTED BY
H. O. HOUGHTON AND COMPANY.

CONTENTS.

—◆—

PROTECTION AGAINST FIRE.

CHAPTER I.

PERSONAL.

NEAR the close of a hot summer day, many years since, the people of Charlestown, Massachusetts, were startled by the cry of " fire." On a small house near the bridge, there was a little fire, perhaps three feet in diameter. An earnest man could have dashed it out in a minute or two, with a pail of water. No one, however, made an attempt to do what every one supposed would be done in a few minutes by the firemen. The firemen did not come as expected, and as there was a high wind, the fire quadrupled its proportions every minute, and soon the flames leaped upon two large buildings, which before the first engine got to work were all on fire. The people now saw their error, but it was too late. ·The engine was powerless, and soon other great buildings were in flames, and a conflagration was imminent. The " little one had become a thousand," and although a few minutes before it could have been smothered

1

with a blanket, or dashed out with a few pails of water, it was now fighting a successful battle with the Charlestown and Boston fire departments. On the wings of the wind, the fire flew over the engines, and soon ten, twenty, and thirty buildings were on fire, which was cutting its fiery way through the town. A dreadful consternation seized upon the people whose homes were in flames, and upon those whose property lay in the direction the fire was flying with awful rapidity. The roaring and crackling of the burning and falling buildings, the shrieks of the affrighted women and children, the yells of the firemen, the cries of the men, and the clang of the bells added to the awful terror, while the water poured into the great hotels and other buildings, only seemed to add to the fury of the fire. Forty, fifty, sixty, and at last seventy buildings, and a great amount of other valuable property were swept away, when by the help of open spaces between the rows of wooden buildings, aided by the great exertions of the firemen, the fire was subdued, but with a loss of more than $200,000.

Amid the confusion of such conflagrations, there are often places which, while the firemen are at work at more important points, must be neglected, and yet where the right man in the right place may save property from destruction. While I was looking about for a chance to help somebody, or something, I saw quite a fire in the out shed of a large three-story house. A good pump, a bucket, a strong arm and a willing mind, made short work of that incipient conflagration. My attention was next directed to the front of the same house. People were removing the furniture from it as the fire was burning a row of wooden houses separated from it only by a narrow street or lane. It occurred to me that the house might be saved, even though the engines could not be spared from other places. I soon told half a dozen men my plan, and in a few minutes there was a tub of water, buckets and dippers, in every room, where the out-side was exposed to the oncoming fire, and a man in each room to open a window and dash out the fire as it caught on the outside, while other men supplied the tubs with the necessary water from the pump. As I could stand fire like a salamander, I volunteered to remain outside, and to point to where the fire caught on the building, and to see that the men were supplied with water.

Soon the fire became terrific, and there was hardly a moment when some window was not opened, and water thrown to dash out the flames. Indeed there was one time when the whole front of the house seemed covered with flames, while from every window flew water from pails and dippers. The glass cracked into thousands of pieces, looking like frost work, but the water from the windows just at the right moment, kept the fiery river at bay. The heat grew less intense, and at last the " Brigade " came together to congratulate themselves upon their success. We met in the parlor, though not in dress suits, for a more wet and tired party of young men it would have been hard to find. My eyes soon gave me notice by their stinging pain to go to the pump which had served us so well, for a bath for them. The clear, cool water, soon made the eyes all right, and I felt like a new man. I was then again called to the parlor to be introduced to the owner of the house. He was one of those stately solid men of Boston, and vicinity, who, alas, have almost passed away. Taking off his hat, he said, " I am told, young man, that under Providence, you have been the means of saving my house from this dreadful fire, and I want to give you my heartfelt thanks for your earnest and successful efforts in my behalf." I think I blushed a little. It was easy to do so after fighting such a battle with fire. But I tried to bear my honors meekly, told him of my " Brigade " who had done such good services, bowed myself out, and was soon on my way home on foot to Watertown, as wet as a rat, as tired as a whole pack of dogs, but as happy as a king.

I never again met the owner, or any of my fire friends who fought it out on that line that night, but I am sure that I then and there learned a lesson which has enabled me to be of some use in the world by preventing fires, and God willing I will hope and strive to do more. From that time I was convinced that it is the duty of every man or woman, boy or girl, to attack and put out fires instantly, when they are small and easily managed, and that when there is a fire and the firemen are not able to defend every exposed place, others should, and often might with the same success which attended our efforts at Charlestown. The fire which I have attempted to describe occurred August 25, 1835.

Since that time, now nearly forty years, I have, with all possible diligence, carefully studied the manner of and the means for extinguishing fires, the careless and reckless manner of erecting buildings, and the danger to towns and cities from spontaneous combustion, inflammable oils, etc.

The result of my observations will be found in the following pages.

CHAPTER II.

OF THE GREAT INCREASE OF FIRES.

THE rapid increase in the number and magnitude of fires in the past few years, seems to many people who have given but little attention to the subject, to be a mystery.

There is something uncanny about it. A gentleman in Chicago, who was at the dreadful fire in that city, told me he had no doubt that its awful magnitude was entirely owing to the electricity with which the air was charged at that time. If well-informed people entertain· such ideas, what may not less intelligent minds be led to conceive?

This subtle element, so useful to mankind when confined within the limits of safety, now so often bursts those bounds, that we may reasonably suppose there is never a moment that there is not somewhere in the United States a fire, more or less destructive in its ravages.

Now, in the city, town, village, hamlet, or on the isolated farm; on the prairie, in the forest, or at the hut of the lonely settler, ever somewhere may be seen the cloud of smoke by day, or the crimsoning sky by night, telling of distress and disaster from this prolific source of evil.

A city has in one of its buildings a tiny fire, which could be hid under a bushel. Neglected, it has burned its way out to the raging gale. Now it rushes on its fiery pathway, through miles of streets, the homes of thousands, to the water's edge, or out to the open country. For weeks we read of the dreadful loss; of the dead, of the sick and wounded, the sufferings of the poor, houseless, and almost starving people; of the startling incidents, the loss of life, the fortunate escapes from fearful peril, the ruin of thousands who, before the fire, were surrounded with comforts; of the calls for aid, the thanks for help received. At length the tale is changed, and we learn of the uprising of new buildings, reared in midwinter, or in a few weeks or days, perhaps more carelessly erected than those so lately destroyed.

A town has been swept out of existence by a little spark lighting upon a roof, out of the reach of those who saw it, and which, fanned by the wind, ran like wild-fire over the dried shingles, which were taken upon a dozen other buildings before the department could be got to work. Another cry for help; another sad account of distress and destitution. Another blessed shower of relief; another outpouring of heartfelt thanksgiving.

The spaces of time between such dreadful disasters are only too well filled up with accounts of the destruction of villages, homesteads, and workshops in every section of the country. Almost all such fires are seen when so small that, with the same coolness and presence of mind with which we attend to other affairs, and with proper implements for extinguishing them, such as we provide for our other work, would be put out in a few minutes, and with so little loss as to hardly be worth telling of to the neighbors.

Thus ever war, and almost every battle is a defeat. A hundred fires of buildings destroyed to one instantly attacked and saved.

Ever reading of disaster, loss of property, often of life, when one occurs we become panic-stricken when we should be more than ever self-possessed.

It should be the duty of some person in every town to give the cause of fires, why they were not at once put out, how large or small they were when first seen, how much they had increased when water was thrown upon them, and if extinguished at once and without loss, the manner and means made known, that other property might be saved in like manner. If such a record was published, we should learn that one cause of fires was the crowding together of wooden buildings, as at Portland and at Chicago, from which sparks flying from the first building on fire, would set many others on fire before the first engine could be got to work, or even perhaps before the telegraph told the firemen there was a fire. And if it should be proved that for these little fires the small hand-engines were more efficient than great steam fire-engines, and that such fires, by their use, could have been put out with a loss of a few dollars instead of many millions, they would soon be adopted. Then by the combined force of the steamers and the small engines, conflagrations would become almost obsolete. Many an awful fire, the news of which has been sent over the land, would have been dashed out without loss by some man or woman, boy or girl, if proper and efficient means for doing it were at hand, and it was the custom to publish such instances of self-possession at fires, as it was of the heroic deeds of the soldiers in our late war.

Take, for instance, the following example: A boy, employed in a store near the Old South Church, discovered a fire in the basement of the store, in a very dangerous place, which in a few minutes would have driven the inmates from the store, and resulted in the loss of thousands of dollars worth of property. Springing to the wash-bowl, the only implement at hand, he filled it with water and throwing it upon the flames, he was in a moment back with another, and others followed, and so he dashed it out almost before the other inmates knew there was a fire on the premises. As one of the salesmen went to find the cause of the smoke and disturbance, the lad emerged from the smoke, saying, as he rushed for more water, "I have got it almost out!" And soon it was quite out, and the serious danger over. Not a word of this praiseworthy action was reported. Yet it would no doubt have prevented many other fires if published and commented upon in the newspapers of the day. Nor do I believe that the boy ever received a "thank you, sir," from the insurance company, for whom he saved thousands of dollars.

The best managed fire I ever saw was dashed out in a few minutes by a woman who worked with entire self-possession, and taught a man and her daughter to do so also. A kettle of tar had boiled over in a wheelwright shop, and set the stock, chips, and shavings under a work bench on fire. The workman now seeing the fire, took the kettle of tar from the fire-place to the door, dropping the burning tar all the way, and throwing it out to the side of the shop, where there was a large hole into the cellar down which the burning tar ran upon the chips and shavings which were scattered about there.

A pretty kettle of — tar one would say! A

dense black smoke enveloped the row of buildings, and gave the alarm to the firewoman. The wind was blowing a gale to add to the danger. In a moment she seized two pails, filled one and telling her daughter to fill the other, and to pump into the trough, she sprang to the fire, and dashed her pail of water under the bench where was the first fire.

In a few seconds came another pail which went into the same place, and drowned out that part of the fire. Now came help, the first man to her assistance. Dashing her next pail of water on the flames along the floor, she pointed to the fire in the cellar, and told him to put it out, which, following her example, he did from the water in the trough, which was now almost full, for the girl stuck to the pump, as her mother did to the fire. By this time the mother had put out all the fire in the shop, and the danger was over, as half a dozen men came rushing up too late to be of any service. If the fire had not been attacked until they arrived, a whole neighborhood would have been destroyed in an hour. Just as the fire was out, though the smoke was so dense that nothing could be seen in the shop, the workman came out of it, as black as a tar-barrel, and with lamp-black enough upon him to have fitted out a dozen negro minstrels!

I doubt if the brave heroine of this exploit was ever thanked by more than one of the half a dozen owners of the buildings in danger, or received a reward from those for whom she saved many thousands of dollars. Nor did the account of the fire go into the papers to teach, and encourage other women and men to follow her example in similar times of danger.

A house far from help from engines took fire on the roof, and before it was discovered a large portion of one side of the roof was on fire. A young lady of the house caught a mop and pail of water, and telling the others to bring more water, she got on the roof, and dashing out the flames with the mop, soon did for the house what Mrs. Partington could not do with the Atlantic Ocean. She mopped out the fire, and saved their pleasant home from destruction. The excellent lesson she taught the world will first be told in this book. If it had been told in the papers of the day, many a fire would have been mopped out, many another home saved.

CAUSES OF FIRE.

The general use of inflammable oils for lighting houses, often sold when it is more dangerous than gunpowder to life and property, the careless manner of setting stoves and funnels and furnaces, the introduction of steam and hot water, and the careless manner of their arrangement for heating buildings, are wholesale causes of the great increase of fires. The construction of buildings, so that if the fire has burned through a partition, ceiling, or stairway, it is out of sight, and with an excellent draft, often better than that of the chimney, it rapidly and safely travels over, and destroys them, is another prolific source of danger.

The introduction into houses and manufactories of chemicals which may take fire from spontaneous combustion, the enormous and careless use of matches, the employment of cheap and careless workmen and watchmen in situations of danger from fires, all add greatly to the number of fires, while the story of the danger of Mansard roofs was told with awful force by the fire at Boston last November.

A very great cause of fires is the wicked recklessness of our people, who will not be taught by such dreadful lessons. Look at the wooden Mansard roofs which have been erected in Boston and vicinity since that great fire. Think of the dreadful fire on Hanover Street where so many lives were lost, and then read in the papers of the hundreds of similar buildings about the city! The general want of knowledge of the best way instantly to attack fires when small and easily extinguished, and an almost entire want of efficient machines for that purpose, and a want of the self-possesssion which persons having them

require, are other causes in the long list. I once
saw where a barn had been burned from the centre
of a nest of buildings, to which the "great box,
little box, band-box, and bundle," would have been
but a feeble comparison. I asked a friend how
they were saved. "Do you recollect lecturing on
fires at the State House once?" said he. "Yes."
"Well, I bought an engine, and soon after, that
barn took fire. It set the buildings on fire on
every side of it, and I, with half a dozen men to
give me water, went right round, dashing out the
flames on one, and then another, and keeping them
wet until the barn burned down; they were all
saved." When I say that my friend was Mr.
Benjamin Cutter, of Pelham, New Hampshire,
the farming portion of my readers will have no
doubt the work was well done.

But the cause, perhaps, more than all others
combined, is the fact that our fire departments
are so arranged that from the time that the fire
is first seen, the telegraph people told of it, the
horses put to the engines, the engines taken to the
fire, then attached to the hydrants, or the reservoirs, and the hose taken to the fire, and the water
is turned on to the fire, is upon an average at least
fifteen minutes; while a fire doubling its proportions at first every minute, and soon quadrupling,
works its way through a building in that time, or

if in a dry time and a gale of wind, has become a conflagration, and as at Portland, Chicago, and Boston, acquired a power which the engines cannot control.

No one who reads this chapter can fail to perceive that the means by which buildings may take fire have been increased much more rapidly than those for arresting the fires. We know that fires are best managed if instantly attacked when small; yet we so arrange our fire fighting systems that they cannot be thus attacked. We say "a stitch in time saves nine," and then do not take the stitch. We say " Light blows kill the devil," but do not strike the light blows ; that " a short horse is soon curried," and wait until our fires are full grown ; that " delay makes the danger," and then always delay. Is it not better to give more attention to this important subject than to wait until more cities, God only knows which they may be, are destroyed. THINK ON THESE THINGS ! And thinking, act upon them.

CHAPTER III.

HOW TO PRESERVE LIFE FROM DESTRUCTION BY FIRE.

SINCE the great fires of the two years past the press has teemed with plans, some wise and many unwise, upon the question of how to prevent fires. But very few words or thoughts for the protection of life from the same danger, have been presented. And yet the value of a life, that is a life worth preserving, cannot be weighed in the same scale with houses and warehouses.

In the large cities and towns, costly means are provided for fighting fires, and many thoughtful persons have provided extinguishers and small engines for preventing them. But neither the large or the small engines can be of any use for saving the life of persons whose clothing has taken fire from the dangerous oils in common use, or from matches, or from stoves or open fire-places.

And yet a knowledge of how to instantly apply means to be found in every house, would prevent almost every catastrophe of this kind. There should be a hearth-rug if possible in every room in the

house in which a fire is kept, an overcoat in the
hall, and blankets or woolen bed clothing in every
bedroom in the house.

The first great requisite of safety is that the
person whose clothing has taken fire should not
lose his presence of mind. Throwing one's self
upon the floor and wrapping a rug or blanket or
overcoat about one, would occupy two or three
seconds, and the danger would be over. The reason for lying down is, that then the flames burn
quite slowly towards a vital part, but almost instantly while standing upright.

If persons awake in the night and find the room
filled with smoke, they should get out of bed and
creep with the face as near the floor as possible
to a door or window. A room may be so full of
smoke as to suffocate any one standing up, and be
perfectly safe to breathe in, a few inches from the
floor. Mr. Braidwood relates the following inci-
dent upon this subject : —

" A fire had broken out in the third floor of a
house, and when I reached the top of the stairs
the smoke was rolling in thick heavy masses,
which prevented me from seeing six inches before
me. I immediately got down upon the floor, above
which for the space of about eight inches the air
seemed to be remarkably clear and bright. I
could distinctly see the feet of the tables and

2

other furniture of the room; the flames in this space burning as vivid and distinct as the flame of a candle, while all above the smoke was so thick that the eye could not penetrate it. The fire had already burnt out of five windows in the apartment, yet when lying flat on the floor, no inconvenience was felt except from the heat."

Never reënter a house on fire from which you have escaped for anything of trifling value. Nothing but the life of some of the family should tempt you to do it; and not then until you have coolly measured the danger. Many lives are lost in the attempt to save others. If you do attempt to save a life, recollect the following rule of the London Fire Brigade. "He (the Superintendent) never allows any man unaccompanied by another to enter a building on fire." The loss of life in the Boston warehouses is a lesson on this subject. Stores and their contents may be constructed or purchased. Life cannot.

THE DANGER FROM LAMPS.

There should be special laws prohibiting the sale of oils made of benzine and similar dangerous substances, which mixed with kerosene is the cause of the loss of so much life and property in the United States. A lady who is careful of and anxious for the safety of her family, said to me, " I

asked for Downer's oil, and was told they did not
sell it. They, however, had a safe oil which would
not explode. They poured some of it into a plate,
and lighting a match, they put it upon the kerosene, which put out the fire on it." And so she
supposed she could use it with perfect safety.
This experiment is performed all over the country
as follows: A fellow of no learning or character
sets himself up in the oil business. His stock in
trade is a barrel of benzine and a gallon of kerosene oil. His oil is a famous new chemical discovery. It will burn more quickly, give more light,
and is more safe than any other, as it is made on
PHILOSOPHICAL PRINCIPLES! And you cannot
explode it if you try to do so all day. Then the oil
is poured on the tin pan or plate, the match applied
to the fluid, and of course the fire is extinguished.
Now for the mystery. Benzine does not explode,
but the vapor which rises from it does. When
the benzine is poured upon the plate the vapor
passes off into the air safely. When it is gone, the
match is applied with the aforesaid result. But
when the dangerous oil is in a lamp, the vapor in
the lamp cannot find its way to the air, but fills
the lamp above the oil. Now we have the flame
of the lamp over the vapor. If we blow the flame
down to the vapor, or so shake the lamp as to force
a tiny stream of the vapor up to the flame, or the

vapor increases until it fills the lamp and is forced up by the side of the wick to the flame, the vapor takes fire and burns its way back into the lamp, when the whole of the vapor explodes, setting fire to the oil. Then the vapor sets fire to and kills the person holding it, and the oil sets fire to the house, which is often also destroyed.

These fires follow the introduction of such " Patent Oils " all over the country where they are sold. The maker of the oil grows rich in a neighborhood, then migrates to another State to follow the same devilish vocation. I know of no punishment worthy of the offense, unless we imitate that of the ancient Romans, and sew him in a sack saturated with his oil and set it on fire.

Never blow down the chimney of a kerosene lamp to extinguish it. Never use great quart lamps. They are very dangerous. If you have them throw them against a stone wall. Never buy the cheapest oil. " Get the best."

Lamps when lighted in the morning without being filled, and taken quickly about the house, are very liable to explode. A neighbor left his house before light in the morning some time ago to do the morning work of the barn. Not long after he heard an explosion, and the bright light in his house told him where was the danger. His wife had risen, and lighting the kerosene lamp, was walking across the room, when it exploded, throwing the burning naphtha over her, and setting her clothing on fire. She was quite near some water which she at once used, and with the help of her husband the fire on her person and on the house was soon out. She was, however, badly burned but her life was saved.

But many people will purchase poor oils, if a few cents cheaper than the best, and accidents will happen in the best of families. A little anecdote with its caution shall therefore end this chapter.

Sometime since I had a conversation upon this subject with a gentleman, who had the good sense to speak of it to his family, and they formed a little Home Fire Brigade. Soon afterwards, a few minutes after one of the young ladies had retired for the night an explosion was heard. The family rushed up-stairs and upon opening the room they found the lamp exploded, but the young lady was " as snug as a bug in a rug," the fire all out and the danger over.

CHAPTER IV.

HOW TO PROTECT OUR HOMES AND WORKSHOPS FROM FIRE.

ALL cities and large towns are said to be "protected" by "fire departments;" but small towns, villages, and the farming population, however much they may be assessed to pay for the town engines, are most of them so far away that the engines are of no use for preventing fires, while they too often see their barns and outhouses destroyed by incendiary fires, set that there may be a "good time."

The common manual engine cannot be distributed in such places, as its house and the engine would be too expensive, and there would not be men enough found to work it, until the fire had burnt out. The popular steam fire-engine for such purposes would be about as useful as an elephant for weeding carrots! There are engines, cheap and efficient, which can be worked by men or women, boys or girls, and which should be purchased by every respectable family in all the length and breadth of the land. But as a vast majority

of our people do not know that there are such
useful machines, and as all are exposed to fires at
any hour, I propose to show that many fires can
be prevented by an earnest application of water
from the common utensils of the house.

A water-pail or two, a pint pot, and an axe,
make a "splendid" apparatus for preventing many
fires. Neither the man who doubts this nor all his
neighbors owns a thousandth part as much property as they have already saved or as much as they
will save, before every person is properly protected
by something better. A short time since, on a
cold, windy day, fire was discovered in a room of
a large house, in which there were two women
only. The room was very much on fire when first
seen. One woman pumped the water, took it to the
other, and begged her to give up the house, and
save what furniture they could, and themselves; the
other dashed the water on the fire as fast and as
well as she could, and encouraged the first to keep
on fighting the fire. The result was that soon the
fire gave in, and retreated into the inside waste
places round the chimney — nice little places from
where fires can work their way out of sight to
every portion of a house. At this time a neighbor,
a fire engineer, arrived, and with a hatchet soon
cut his way into the fire, when a dipperful or two
of water dashed it out, and the hatchet was again

put to work. He knew the efficiency of small engines, and, said he, "when I went to work, I would have given a hundred dollars for one." There were plenty of them only a third of a mile away. A man was sent to give word to the steam-engine, two miles away, and to get the small ones. He was a man of great ideas, and so sent for the steamer, and neglected the small ones. But the engineer's pail, hatchet, and dipper waited for nothing. Crack went the hatchet, and slap went water from the dipper, and in ten minutes or so he had the satisfaction of resting, and thinking that his neighbors, through his noble efforts, had not been turned houseless into the streets on one of the coldest days of the winter. The same kind of courage as that of the women and man, the same simple little implements as well applied, would prevent a great portion of the fires which now afflict our country. The great steamer was hurried down in time to find the fire out, and the people quietly about their usual avocations. Some years ago, a fire caught in the wood-box of a small house, and an alarm was soon given to the neighborhood, where, at one of the houses, a small engine was kept. In the room on fire, the clothes of a washing were hung up and were dried. They caught, and burned like tinder. The fire had charred the whole room, and nearly burned through the partitions. Two men of good sense came toward the fire from one side, and a young woman with an engine from the other. The men, with plenty of water at hand, dashed it out just as the engine was ready to do so. Here were two ways, to " choke a cat " to prevent a fire. Either could have done it, if the other had not been tried, while the house would have burned up before the great engines of the town, two miles away, could have known anything about it.

Many years ago a fire was discovered in a woolen mill near Boston. The neighbors rallied, and thinking it could not be saved, they went to work with a will to save such property as they could reach. One of those people who look and think as well as work, came in, and looking about, he cried out, " Hold on here ! Let us put out this fire, and then we shall have plenty of time to take out the goods !" In a minute he had them fighting the fire, and in a short time it was out. It was then quite as much work to return the goods as it had been to extinguish the fire !

Some years ago, a house was set on fire near Mount Auburn. It was a new, unfinished house, and one of the rooms of the first story was in a roaring, blazing fire when it was discovered. The first man who got to the fire caught hold of the nice new pump in the kitchen and wrenched it off !

But where there is a will there is a way, and soon a dozen men were engaged in throwing water from a neighboring ditch upon the fire, with pails. Fire is a great coward, and gets out of the way of such deluges as quick as possible, and this one did not get into any room but that in which it was discovered. Some time after the people who put the fire out, had got home, and to bed, an engine or two came rushing from the neighboring city. The fire was out long before they had got the alarm. The pump was brought back safely the next morning. The man who " put the pump out," was soon afterward chosen one of the fire-wards! At the next fire in the neighborhood, it was a raw cold morning, and the fire was set in a great barn. The neighbors got tubs and pails of water and placed them so as to throw the water upon the house, if it should get warm, and then went nearer to the fire to keep themselves from freezing. When lo! our fire officer came rushing up, mounted the roof of the house and threw water for a long time on it, where it froze as fast as it fell. Such people are found at every country fire. I once saw a person go to work on a great shed with an axe to cut it in two! He could have done his work in about a week, and with a scarf twenty feet wide. The fire soon drove him off. But there is a bright side also. I never yet went to a fire in the country, that I did not find numbers of people willing to work, and who worked with a will, and also with judgment.

If a house takes fire around a chimney, get your axe or hatchet and a pail of water and tell the people to bring a pint pot, and then go to work quickly, for the smoke will drive you out if your work is not soon finished. A few blows with the axe and a pint or two of water, and so on; the axe and the water will make short work of quite a fire. A fine large house was observed to have smoke in the upper rooms, and upon examination fire was found in the partition, set from the chimney. Fire! was cried, and the people soon filled the house. All could see where the fire was, and its crackling could be heard. Yet no one suggested an axe to enable the water to be got upon it. Soon the smoke drove them away, when they cleared the house, and waited for the steamer. When this had arrived, the fire had burned the upper half of the house, and as there was no water for the steamer or other great engines, the fire made short work of the other half. The people and the firemen of that village looked on at its destruction, never once supposing that the fire preventive arrangements in that town were not perfect! Many long years since, a farmer on his way to Boston with a load of wood, on a cold, windy morning, when the ther-

mometer was at zero, saw a small light before him.
As he approached, it grew larger, and he saw it
was a house on fire on the roof, a long distance before him.   Leaving his team to follow as it would,
he ran on to alarm the family ; soon he saw something white flying about the roof of the house, and
before he arrived, the something white took the
form of the old man of the house, who in the
smallest possible amount of clothing, had got upon
the roof and was dashing the water, brought by the
family to him, upon the fire.   The fire wilted, and
a bundle of shingles and a few boards was all that
was required to repair the house.   By the time the
farmer had helped the " man in white " to empty
a mug of cider, the wood team came along and the
farmer went off with it, — a better fireman for
what he had seen that night.   These examples of
how buildings may be saved when on fire without
engines, should prompt every person, male or
female, to instantly attack fires.   Thousands of
houses are burned every year, which could have
been put out in a few minutes, and with the loss of
a few dollars, if they had been earnestly fought
with the common pails of the house for weapons.

The excitement, terror, and confusion attending
fires would be almost entirely prevented, if every
person would at once do what they could to help
extinguish a fire.

There is no more danger when working at a fire than there is from any other kind of earnest hard work. And there is no place where an ardent effort is likely to be more successful than when fighting fire.

A few minutes' cool and well directed hard work has often saved many thousands of dollars.

No person will save a house by his or her earnest work without teaching others, who will also be successful if placed in like trying circumstances. Many years ago my father woke up in the night, and found the room full of smoke. He called FIRE up the stairs, and then found the fire in a closet, and put it out with a few pails of water. About fifteen minutes afterwards, his apprentice, nineteen years old, came down the stairs nicely dressed and ready for a day's work. Father dressed himself after he had put out the fire. If he had not, the apprentice might have been burned to death, as he slept just over the fire.

A nurse had come to the house that day, who took up the wood ashes, and placed them in a wooden bucket, which she put in a closet. She was a pretty good nurse for mother and the baby, but a wonderful person to nurse a fire, as this little story illustrates.

A DWELLING-HOUSE SAVED FROM DESTRUCTION.

It was washing-day, and the washing was almost over, when the good lady, as she was taking out a basket of clothes for the line, saw smoke coming down the stairway from the upper portion of the house. Dropping her basket, she rushed up to see what caused it, and found one of the rooms on fire near the chimney. Flying down to the wash-room, she caught a pail, filled it with water from a wash-tub, and in half a minute from the time she saw the smoke, she had dashed the water upon the fire. This was followed by another, and then the hatchet came into use, and one more pail of water, and there was a clearing up of the room, as the fire was out. The agent for the insurance company said to me that he had not the slightest doubt that had the woman left the house and given a fire-alarm, before the engine could have got there and at work, the fire would have insured the total destruction of the building. The damage was only about five dollars.

KEROSENE FIRE PUT OUT.

In the same town, a very careful domestic over-turned a kerosene lamp, which broke on the floor, and set the oil instantly all ablaze. She gave the alarm, when the " man of the house," with most unsuitable clothes to parade the street with, entered the room, and seizing the blanket from the bed, he smothered the fire in a moment or two; then, while putting on his pants, he had the happiness of thinking he had saved about $10,000 as quick, as easy, and with as little clothing on, as ever was done by any other man!

If people, when they discovered such fires, would follow the example of these persons, there would be very few fires indeed. The fires, when so small, are extinguished with the greatest ease; yet the same fire, in a few minutes more, would have got over the rooms and into the ceilings, and destroyed the buildings.

In 1757, while General Putnam was at Fort Edward, the barracks took fire and were destroyed. They were within twelve feet of the magazine, containing three hundred barrels of gunpowder. Putnam took a position between the fire and the magazine, where he could throw water upon it. The building and its dangerous contents were saved. The brave officer was so badly burned that all the skin peeled from his hands, and he was sick for a month. In the times before fire departments were originated, such deeds of bravery were not uncommon; nor are they now, where there are no fire brigades, or where engines fail to arrive in season to protect property in danger.

This was proved at the great Boston fire, where Mr. Pratt saved his house, and at Hovey's store, and at the fire fight on Oliver Street. But when departments were organized, and great engines procured, the people left the work to the firemen, which they could often have better done themselves, and little fires which some one, imitating the brave Putnam, could have extinguished in a few minutes, sometimes destroyed whole villages or towns. Now the young soldier could have been shielded from the awful heat by a door or wide board placed between him and the fire, as is now often done by firemen ; and if he could have had a small engine, he could have saved the property with but little danger. As he did his duty without means, we should learn to do all our duty with them, and fires of considerable magnitude would then be instantly dashed out.

CHAPTER V.

BEFORE describing a new preventive system, let us see if there are such faults in the old as to make it so inefficient as to require a change. Take the Boston Fire Department for an example. The people of Boston, having adopted a system, have spared no expense to make it as perfect as possible. Men, horses, and engines are as good as can be found. If anything is wrong, it is in the system alone. The evils attending it are its tendency to show, its great expense, and its inefficiency. The last is the important objection, and let us see how great it really is.

A fire is discovered; in the confusion, a minute or two is lost before any one is sent to give the alarm. The average time to run to the nearest box is two minutes; to find the person who has the key, tell him where the fire is, and for him to open the box and give the alarm, two minutes more. There is no doubt that the time from when the fire is seen until the telegraph tells three hundred thousand people that there is a fire, averages

five minutes. Next, the horses are attached to
the engines in one or two minutes, when the first
engine is taken to the fire in from three to five
minutes, the engine attached to the hydrant, and
the leading hose taken to the fire in five minutes
more. Five minutes·to telegraph, five to harness
and get to the fire, and five more to get water
upon the fire, or at least fifteen minutes is lost,
upon an average, from the time a fire is discovered
before water is thrown upon it. Now, if the fire
would wait fifteen minutes, the only result of the
delay would be that the great engines would cause
a great waste and loss by water. They would
always put out the fire, but the water loss would
be a serious one.

But the fire is seldom so accommodating. It
burns on, always doubling its proportions every
minute, and often in dangerous places quadrupling
its proportions every minute.

If it has doubled each minute for the fifteen,
the result is a great loss by fire and water. If it
has quadrupled, it is a total loss of the building on
fire; and if there is added to that crowded and
dangerous buildings and a high wind, there is a
dreadful conflagration.

Such has been the history of the Boston department since the introduction of steam fire-engines.
The Fourth of July fire at East Boston was so

small, when first seen, that a man took a pail, to
which was attached a cord, to fill from the wharf,
and with the water he would have extinguished the
fire, but the cord untying, the bucket floated away,
and the loss by fire in five hours was half a million
of dollars. This is one example. The turret fire,
also at East Boston, of which the president of the
company making the turrets for war vessels waiting for them at the Navy Yard, said to me: "I
could have covered the fire with my hat if I could
have reached it, or have put it out with one of
your engines in a minute! The loss was $250,000,
besides the loss of the use of the iron-clads for a
year. Still another was the destruction of the
Winthrop House and Masonic Temple, of which
the police reported that, when they arrived (not
when the fire was first seen), it could have been
easily put out with a few buckets of water. And
who does not recollect the great fire which began
in a hay-store near the Boston and Maine Depot, and
which for a time was one of the most splendid fire
battles ever fought by the Boston firemen. The
men worked like heroes; the splendid engines
almost outdid themselves. But the fire rushed on
through the hay and straw stores and the stables,
then on to the great depot on one side, and the
rows of wooden buildings filled with numerous
families on the other, while a great cloud of smoke

rolled over the city, from which dropped millions of sparks, one of which set fire away off on Charles Street. Firemen fell into the flames, but were taken out without a loss of life. Many thousands of dollars worth of property were destroyed. Who seeing that terrible battle could have believed that this monstrous fire, when first seen, was so small, only on one bundle of hay, and that within a few feet of the door, out of which it could have been pitched in a moment, or the fire dashed out with a small engine in two seconds!

These are a few of the many instances of the inefficiency of the present system under the most favorable circumstances, for the department of Boston is one of the best in the world.

But why has not this inefficiency been discovered before? Just as the streets of Boston have continued narrow and crooked. Just as the Boston Board of Health nursed the small-pox until the people would not longer endure the nuisance, and so turned reformers. Just as the London Fire Brigade, when Ericsson, our turret hero, with John Braithwaite of London, made a splendid steam fire-engine in 1829, did all they could to annoy its workmen, and would not, if possible, allow it to play at fires. Of this we have the following account:—

" This engine worked with the greatest success

at the fire at the Argyll Rooms, when the cold was so severe that the manual engines quickly became frozen and useless, but the steamer worked incessantly for five hours without a hitch, throwing its stream clear over the dome of the building, at St. Charles Street, Soho, at the burning of the English Opera-house, and Messrs. Barclay's brewery, besides many others of less magnitude, at all of which it rendered signal service in preventing the fire from spreading. For these gratuitous services and the great outlay encountered by Mr. Braithwaite, he received but little patronage and support from the general public; and from the insurance companies, who must have been benefited some thousands of pounds by his exertions, he received the magnificent testimonial, presented to his men, of *one sovereign!* In short, the managers of the Fire Brigade declined to entertain Mr. Braithwaite's proposals, and their servants, when they met him with his engine at fires, which he for a long time attended gratuitously, perpetrated every possible annoyance towards him, so that he ultimately withdrew in disgust from the new field in which he had hoped to have both profitably and usefully employed his talents and resources."

These are the reasons! And such have been the reasons why every improvement has been opposed in all times. But if the present steamers are not sufficient, why not add more? Well, double the number, and see the result. The same time to hesitate, to run to the telegraph box, to attach the horses, to attach the hydrant, and get the leading hose out to the fire; a minute or two saved in running to the fire; so that were the expense increased to a million of dollars annually, the efficiency for *preventing* fires would be but slightly increased. For fighting them, if the water supply was sufficient (as it is not), they would be more efficient, of course. But do not forget that preventing and not fighting fires is what we most need. The fires of Chicago and Boston prevented, would have saved nearly $300,000,000.

No person who reads the daily papers can fail to notice the great number of persons who are killed in one way or another by pistol shots. A ball from one of these little instruments will as effectually kill a man as will a six or a sixty pound shot, and in a much more decent manner. Now the same degree of intelligence and ingenuity which has been devoted to the weapons for destroying man, has been expended upon little machines for extinguishing fire. In this country where the one great idea for years has been to throw the largest stream of water, we don't understand this.

But small engines were introduced into the London Fire Brigade in 1848, since which time one has always been attached to the great engines. When they reached the fire, it was fought, if large, by the great engine, but if small, a great fire was prevented by the little one, and with only a slight loss by water.

Let us now learn the English opinion of these little machines, after fifteen years' experience. Mr. Charles E. King, C. E., in a paper upon the suppression and extinction of fires read before the London Society of Arts, in 1863, said: " From the great apparent difficulty of successfully dealing with large fires, it is manifest that those plans will be most advantageous which can be applied at the commencement of a fire. And for this purpose, the ordinary hand pump cannot be surpassed. The great success which has attended its use both by firemen and civilians, is in many well authenticated cases truly marvelous. Many fires which upon their first discovery could have been covered with a hat, for want of such an apparatus as a hand pump and a pail of water, have grown into extensive conflagrations."

In the discussion which followed the reading of Mr. King's paper, the experienced Mr. Baddely said: " In its early stages, fire in most cases is quite manageable, and that is the time when it can be dealt with, with the greatest chances of success. Of all modern inventions for fire extin-

guishing purposes, nothing in my opinion is so
really useful as the little hand pump.   Many years
of controversy ensued before the late Mr. Braidwood could be brought to regard the hand pump
with favor.   The result of the experiments with
the little hand engines was so satisfactory, that
every fire-engine in London travels with one ; and
they have been the means, in the hands both of
firemen and civilians, of saving thousands of
pounds worth of property."

The " experienced Mr. Baddely " had no doubt
given more attention to fire apparatus than any
person in Europe or America.   He had taken out
twenty-two patents for new engines or fire apparatus.   He designed the cabinet fire-engine for the
Duke of Bedford's picture gallery, at Belvoir Castle, great numbers of which have come into use in
England ; the farmer's engine, the portable fire-
engine, adopted by the London Fire Brigade, and
by Mr. Braidwood in 1848.

In 1858, Mr. Braidwood wrote of them after ten
years' experience ; " There should be a tank on the
top of each staircase," he was writing of the great
London warehouses, " with six fire buckets, and
three small pumps.   The officers and work people
seeing them every day, would be certain to run to
them in case of fire, and small accidents might be
extinguished at once, and the iron doors and
roofs kept cool in case of one room taking fire."

This advice was unheeded, and on a pleasant morning in 1861 a slight smoke was seen rising from a pile of hemp. The " officers and workmen " had nothing to work with, and before the firemen arrived, the fire had got so far into the great warehouses, that all the Fire Brigade with the great river steam-engines, throwing thousands of gallons of water per minute, could not extinguish it for a fortnight. The loss of merchandise, etc., was $11,-000,000. But worst of all, Mr. Braidwood, whose advice, if followed, would have probably prevented the fire, was himself crushed to death by the falling of the walls, thrown down by an explosion of saltpetre.

From " Fires, Fire Engines, etc.," we take the following description of the " London Pump." " It is now a force pump easily worked by one person, so that an efficient and very compact miniature fire-engine is the result. It will throw about six gallons of water per minute thirty feet and upwards, in a strong and continuous stream, and by directing the water on the fire, it will soon knock out what, if left a few minutes longer, would almost always end in a disastrous conflagration. These hand pumps are extensively used in London, and in the late Lambeth Fire Brigade, and they are extensively used by those in the country, their convenience and advantages being proved to be beyond question. It is a remarkable fact that while at the great conflagration in Tooley Street in 1861 (where Mr. Braidwood was killed), the steam engines were pouring tuns of water per minute into the burning buildings, without producing the slightest effect, Beal's Wharf was saved, and the progress of the flames eastward averted, by means of a hand pump. There can be no doubt that had there been a few of these little pumps at hand when the great fire in Gresham Street was first discovered by the watchmen, their employment with a few gallons of water would have prevented the great destruction of property that ensued."

This fire in Gresham Street, was a carpet warehouse and contents, and the loss was $900,000.

In connection with the statement of the fire at Tooley Street, where the fire was kept from Beal's Wharf by a little engine, it seems proper to give an account of a similar instance which took place in Boston, at the great fire on Fort Hill, July 10, 1852. The fire was seen when it was on an old stable in an alley way leading from Belmont Street. It was so small when seen, and the alarm given, that a man, one of the engineers of the Boston Fire Department, who was present, said of it to me, " I could have covered it with the shawl on your arm, if I could have reached it, or put it out in half a minute with your pump." It was, however, out of his reach, on a low stable, which could have been reached by the water from the pump. There was a high wind, and the fire spread with fearful rapidity by the burning wood flying over and lighting on buildings some distance from the main fire. For a time there were fears that a large portion of the city would be destroyed. The fire burned the Sailor's Home, and the Boylston School-house, but its greatest fury was spent in a great number of large buildings, each of which was crowded with numbers of poor families.

The scene at the fire therefore was fearful. The women and children screaming — the heaps of furniture thrown into the streets, impeding the firemen, until they took fire and burned up, the falling buildings, and the roar of the flames, spread terror through all but the firemen, who never gave way for a moment, and who after five hours' work arrested the fire, but not until nearly sixty buildings were swept away. In the time of greatest confusion, when the furious conflagration was sweeping down upon a large three-story wooden building, at the head of one of the wharfs on which were buildings containing United States bonded goods of great value, and the wooden building had taken fire on the outside from the intense heat, and there was not an engine to be had at any sacrifice, as all were holding the fire at other places, a man exclaimed, " I can put that fire out with our little engine ! Where is it ? In the stable. Bring it ! In a moment he brought a little rotary pump, which, made in New York, had been sent to Boston and exhibited in Congress Street, where persons were invited to try it. How often had I done that. And oh, how I wanted that engine ! How I worked it, and saw what it would do to save my house at Watertown if it caught fire, before the great engines could get news of the fire, and run two miles to us ! But it is money which makes engines as well as mares go, and I never had the money to buy it, and it was now at this fire, in order, and close to this great wooden house on fire on the outside. It was in the upper story in a minute, and a stream of water thrown back upon the house soon dashed off the fire, and then the water thrown upon the highest part of the house trickled down to the bottom of the house, and so the entire wharf was made perfectly safe ! The engine was played until the fire had burned past. That little engine saved all the property on that wharf, and it would have prevented the great fire of November from spreading to the second store, and would have saved in buildings, merchandise, and loss of time, etc., more than $100,000,000. This assertion will be likely to make some of my readers doubt all I have said. But go with me to Hovey's store. See the dreadful fire opposite! See the flames, throwing an intense heat across the street, and the store just ready to break out into another fire to add to the awful conflagration. But look again! See, the Mansard roof is covered with blankets, and look now! See the water thrown upon them! The fire grows more intense, and it is almost impossible to throw the water there! But look again! See that young man out on the roof in the fiery air! Now he can reach every part of that roof, and they give him all the water he needs. The fire is hotter, his cheeks blister, his eyes almost scorch, but the brave man never falters a moment! Steadily the water is thrown on one and another part of the roof, and at last the store is safe and the hero creeps down from his dangerous position, where a false step, or a slip would have sent him to the street a mangled corpse. But the store is saved, and his only loss is a face completely blistered on the side exposed to the fire! That Fort Hill engine, or any of the little ones now on sale, with eight or ten feet of hose, would have saved the store, with one tenth part of the water used, and without any one out on the roof. Still you doubt this. But is it not worth while to see if it is true. Mr. Baddely said, " the results of the *experiments* with the little hand-engines was so satisfactory," etc. So would they be here.

But I have not yet done with English testimony
in favor of small engines. I entreat my readers to
read every word of it, for it is my full belief that
the safety of our cities and large towns for the
future will depend vastly more upon the question of
their introduction than upon any other. " In nearly
every fire in a dwelling-house, whilst the people
are within and awake, there can be no reason to
doubt, that if a simple and ready means of sup-
pressing the fire at its first start were at hand, and
used directly, most of the disastrous conflagrations
which are almost of daily occurrence would never be
heard of. If the records of the various volunteer
and paid fire brigades be inspected, the remark
will continually be found, " extinguished with hand
pumps," by which it will be seen that even after
the time required to give the alarm and fetch the
engine has elasped, the fire has often been put out
by a squirt and a bucket or two of water. As a
rule, it will be found that we trust too much to
other people, and too little to ourselves to subdue
any fire. . . . . Could any arrangement insure
the application of water to a fire of the usual description within the first five minutes of its commencement, the progress of two thirds of them
would be effectually resisted." Words of wisdom
from which we may learn wisdom if we will. It
will be seen that the small engines were only carried

by the brigade on the large engines, and could not be got to the fire and at work under ten or fifteen minutes. The great idea with them is to have them at work in five or ten minutes, but the plan I am about to propose, will have one at work in one, and several in case of need in two or three minutes.

And now for American testimony in favor of little engines. It is not as easily found as in England, for we have been educated for fighting, and not for preventing fires. An acre of raging fire, and a dozen steam fire-engines fighting it, is a glorious sight to most of us. But the Chicago and the Boston fires have been too much for us, and we now occasionally hear that " we are getting it a little too strong," which gives a hope that we may before long have and use a *preventive system.* The " Scientific American," the best paper in the United States to examine and answer such questions, in the number for July 22, 1871, says, " A quick practical means of extinguishing fires at their commencement, on hand, ready for immediate use in every building, would lessen the destruction of property by fire to an extent difficult to estimate. The rule is that the beginnings of fires are small and their progress comparatively slow. In most cases a very little water judiciously applied will extinguish a fire within five minutes of its ignition.

It is for this reason that small portable hand forcing pumps have been approved by the most experienced firemen, as the very best means, all things considered, for extinguishing fires." It also calls the attention of manufacturers to these pumps, and hopes many fortunes will be made by the sale of them for so good a purpose."

From the " American Artisan " we copy from Henry Ward Beecher's sermon, the day of the Boston fire. " The disaster might teach the folly of heaping story on story not fire-proof. How sensible! First a story of granite, then another of granite, then a third of granite, then a fourth of granite, and then — a Mansard roof. Admirable for business, everybody says. Yes, and admirable for fires. Splendid buildings, with an invitation to the fire-devil on every roof. The disaster should also show how needful it is *that every business house should have a supply of water — a fire department for itself.*"

Just what I want, only that *every business house will not have it, and if they once procured it many of them would neglect it.* Therefore I would make it the duty of the cities to furnish it and to keep it in order, when the people, on seeing the fire, will put it out for their own safety, their self-interest.

The "Artisan " also says editorially: " When a fire occurs, somebody has always been either care-

less, ignorant, or imprudent. In erecting buildings, laying out streets, handling or storing merchandise, *constructing fire apparatus*, and in all
that pertains to the origin, prevention, and com-
bating of fires, we are dealing with well-known
and uniform physical and chemical laws. If we
have neglected to heed those laws, and suffered the
consequences, let us own it frankly, and seek to
profit by the lesson. Let us apportion both blame
and praise where they justly belong, and leave to
old women the notion that when fires fail to be extinguished, or stoves don't work well, it is owing
to some mysterious condition of the air."

But if we have not as much home testimony, it
is as good as can be found. Mr. John L. Hayes,
Secretary of the National Association of Wool
Manufacturers, and editor of their " Quarterly
Bulletin," prepared a few years since a paper for
his " Bulletin," entitled, " Fires in Woolen Mills,
their Causes, and Means of Prevention and Extinction." It was found to be so useful that it was
published by itself, and thus many copies were distributed through the country. A friend procured
a copy for me, and hardly ever did I receive such
pleasure from a work as from that. Much of it was
new to me, and all was good. It of course makes
a specialty of that which he wrote about, — woolen
mills, but as the almanacs say, it will answer for

4

any other buildings. There was but one fault with
it: it was published for a few people, and not for
sale. The great mass who so much need the
knowledge, would never get it. I shall therefore
use it, because it will, if known, do good to
others. The first music-book ever published in
Germany, which contained lessons for children, and
music suited for them, so that they could learn to
read music, was not written in the German lan-
guage! So of Mr. Hayes' pamphlet. The great
number to whom it would be useful would never
see it. Mr. Hayes published the extracts from
King and Baddely on this question of small engines, and soon after he had an opportunity to
practically see the usefulness of such means of extinguishing fires.   ·

In the "Bulletin" of April 1872, he says: "Since
the publication in a former number of our article
on 'Fires in Woolen Mills,' the subject has never
been lost sight of. At the time we wrote, we
thought the most practical suggestion contained in
our article was the following." Then he repro-
duces the extract from C. E. King and the remarks
of Baddely, and he says: "Shortly after the article
referred to, our attention was called to a pamphlet
published in 1858, by Mr. Joseph Bird of Mount
Auburn, Mass., entitled 'Fires and Fire-sys-
tems,' and we formed the personal acquaint-

ance of Mr. Bird. This gentleman has been for many years an enthusiastic investigator of the causes of fires and methods of extinction, and possesses more theoretical and practical knowledge of the subject than any person whom we have ever met.

" Mr. Bird, in his pamphlet, thus speaks of the small engines or hand-pumps, which he compares to small arms in the hands of light infantry, steam-engines being compared to light artillery.

" 'But what are the small and the light artillery engines?' First, *small* engines. Any force-pump which one man, woman, or boy can work, and which will force twelve gallons of water per minute through twenty feet of hose and a three-eighth inch pipe, will answer. . . . . ' These simple machines will be found large enough to subdue much the largest portion of our fires. But who will work them? The people who have buildings on fire, and their neighbors. Will they not be too much frightened to work them? They are frightened with the present system, for they have no means at hand for their protection. Can anything be more appalling? A fire in your house, the engine is not, and cannot come for some time to your aid. The fire takes possession of each room and story, and you have before you a blazing mass of flame; and your house, your castle, the home of your loved ones, is destroyed. What can be more frightful? How would you feel, if suddenly beset by a couple of savage dogs, when you had no means of repelling them? How different you would feel, if, just as they were about to spring upon you, you could clutch a club in one hand, and in the other a revolver! How you would make the fur fly! So would a man feel and act if, when he had discovered a fire, he had at hand the means of putting it out."

The following is the testimony which Mr. Hayes gave in an important patent case in court: —

"A little hand-pump, costing not more than from ten to twenty dollars, which could be managed by one man, is regarded by fire engineers as the most valuable of modern inventions for extinguishing fires, because it may be applied at the first moment it is seen. This is also the principal element of the value of the modern fire extinguisher. Expensive fixed apparatus is placed in most modern mills for the same reason. I refer to the apparatus called sprinklers. In the numerous experiments which have been made in Europe and this country to determine the comparative value of steam fire-engines, rapidity of time with which the steam can be got up to work the engines, is generally set down as the first element of comparison. Fires as a rule extend after ignition, in a constantly accelerating ratio as to the time which elapses from the first moment of ignition, partly from the multiplication of centres of ignition, and partly from the development of inflammable gases. Every minute saved at a conflagration in providing the means of extinction is regarded by fire engineers as of the utmost importance. This expresses my opinion as to the value of time."

Mr. Hayes also says: " Since the above was in type, Mr. Bird has kindly consented to perform some experiments, for the special purpose of enabling us to speak, from actual observation, of the efficiency of the small engines. The experiments which we witnessed were made at Mount Auburn. Three old resin barrels, partly filled with shavings, were fully ignited. The fire was almost instantly extinguished with less than a bucket of water, thrown by one of Johnson's pumps. Twelve resin barrels, placed in a pile, and thoroughly ignited, making an intense flame, were as rapidly extinguished by a hand-engine of Mr. Bird's, of somewhat greater power than Johnson's, but easily carried or operated by one man. Finally, a temporary building, made of boards thoroughly dried, the building being about ten feet long, six wide, and twelve high, containing two old resin barrels and a shelf covered with shavings, upon which had been poured a quart of kerosene, was set on fire. When the flames were at full height, a stream from Mr. Bird's hand-engine extinguished the fire in less than a minute. Comment upon these facts is superfluous." Recollect that Mr. Hayes wrote this, not for the public, but for the business men who own and manage the woolen mills of the country. He also says of the Johnson pumps: "Every mill should have at least two of these pumps on each floor." And again: "So sanguine and earnest are we in this advice, that we declare it to be, in our opinion, the most important practical suggestion which has ever appeared in the pages of this Bulletin."

Possibly some reader may say, Mr. Hayes and Mr. Bird mutually admire each other. I cannot answer for Mr. Hayes, but Mr. Bird most certainly admires him, and hopes that so far as the idea of extinguishing fires is concerned it is mutual. And we have a right to respect each other, for we are almost alone in this great war for the safety of our country from fires.

Mrs. Lydia Maria Child lately wrote to me : —

"I am glad you are interesting yourself for the general introduction of garden engines, which I consider a blessing to any neighborhood. A few years ago our house took fire, and the L portion of it was nearly consumed. The whole house must have gone, if there had not been three or four garden engines in the neighborhood, which were promptly brought to the rescue. These kept jets of water continually playing upon the main body of the house and upon the roof, and thus got the fire under control, and finally extinguished it. I have ever since felt a lively gratitude to the inventor of these little and useful machines."

If every person whose house or other buildings have been saved by buckets, small engines, or by snow in winter — for many fires have been kept from spreading into conflagrations by this means, — could tell the stories of their success, it would need nothing else to change our present method. We should at once employ every possible method which could put out a fire. I have known several houses prevented from taking fire by snowballing them until the fires opposite had burned out. Snow, also, while lying on roofs and other exposed places, is one of the best possible protections from fire. A house was once found on fire in the first story, and the pump was frozen and no water could be found. It was filled half full of snow in five minutes, and the fire "snowed out."

But let us see what James Braidwood, of the London Fire Brigade, says : —.

" It has often been a matter of surprise that so small a portion of the public attention should be directed to the matter of extinguishing fires. It is only when aroused by some great calamity that people bestir themselves, and then there is such a variety of plans proposed to avert similar cases of distress, that to attempt to concoct a rational plan out of such a crude, ill-digested, and contradictory mass of opinion, requires more labor than most people are inclined to give to it," etc.

" If the whole experience of the country were brought together and maturely considered, and digested by persons competent to judge, I have no doubt that a system might be introduced suitable to the nation and to the age in which we live. Instead of hearing of '*dreadful loss by fire,*' and the '*great exertions*' made to extinguish it, all the notice would be, — ' Such a place took fire ; the engines arrived, and it was extinguished.'

" It would be useless for me to enter into the details of a plan which I have little hope of ever seeing realized."

It will be seen, from these quotations from the superintendent of the London Fire Brigade, first, that he is surprised people give so little attention to the best manner of extinguishing fires ; second, that he believed a system could be arranged which would prevent dreadful losses by fire; and third, that he had little hope of seeing it accomplished.

I propose to show why he could not bring about the result he so much wished to accomplish.

THE LONDON FIRE BRIGADE.

In 1774 Parliament enacted a law requiring each parish of the city of London to procure and maintain two fire-engines, to be under the charge of the beadles and the parish engineer. The number of these engines was more than three hundred. In the course of time, they were allowed to get out of repair, and otherwise out of order. They were too small to be of much service at great fires, and too large to be got at work in time to put out a fire when first seen.

The insurance companies interested in the safety of the city, aware of the inefficiency of the parish engines, purchased each two engines. There was no superintendent, and each engine went and came from fires at its pleasure.

In 1833 all the engines of the companies were organized into the London Fire Brigade, and placed under the direction of Mr. James Braidwood, who then gave up the charge of the Edinburgh Fire Brigade.

Under his excellent care this brigade became one of the most efficient in the world. In 1855 there were thirty-six engines, each drawn by two horses and capable of discharging about eighty gallons of water per minute, or about two thirds the power of the Hunneman engines of this country. They were kept in nineteen stations, the force of men were one hundred and twelve, and there were forty horses. Only twenty of the engines could be taken to a fire at once or until other horses were procured. The men were always at the stations. When the engines arrived at the fire, men to work the brakes were taken from the crowd, and they received as compensation a shilling for the first hour and sixpence for every other hour they worked. In 1848 a hand pump was attached to each large engine, and when they arrived at the fire, if small, it was put out by the pump, and if large, the others were put to work.

There was no telegraph, and no bells were rung; so when one of the police, or a pieman, or a cabman, or any one else saw a fire, they ran off to the nearest station to tell the firemen. The first person who told them was paid a shilling. Then the firemen got ready to start for the fire, harnessed their horses, when they drove off at a break-neck pace for the fire. One of the directions to the London police will best show the folly of the London fire-alarm system: "Upon any watchman discovering a fire, he shall call the neighboring watchman to his assistance, and shall take the best means in his power to put all concerned upon their guard, and shall immediately send off notice to the nearest office and engine-house. The watchman who is dispatched to give these intimations shall run as far as he can, and shall then send forward any other watchman whom he may meet, he himself following at a walk to communicate his information, in case of any mistake on the part of the second messenger." Every city in the United States would be destroyed in a year if we had so ridiculous a system of fire-alarm. Nothing but the English fogs, and the better, safer manner of building in that country could save them. See in your mind's eye a portly Charley running half a mile, and then hunting up another, and putting him upon the run, perhaps to find a third when he had run out! Now, suppose a little engine at the fire for the first man who saw it to throw water upon it. If a pail or two of water then would not extinguish it, the whole brigade could not when called in that foolish manner.

Mr. Braidwood also says: "The firemen are drilled first daily, and then two or three times a week for some months; and this, with an average of three calls a day, soon makes them acquainted with the routine of their business. But it takes years of constant work to make a good fireman!" One would suppose so, after a fire had been at work as long as it would be from that method of giving an alarm.

But hear Mr. Braidwood again: "When water

is scarce, mud, cow or horse dung, damp earth, etc., may be used as substitutes; but if there seems to be no chance of succeeding by any of these, and the fire is likely to extend to other buildings, the buildings next to the fire should be pulled down." Quite a portion of Chicago was saved by covering one building with wet sand, and another was saved by the careful use of a barrel of cider after the water gave out. Perhaps the best use the State police could make of some of the vile stuff they sometimes pour into the streets would be to pour it upon houses so exposed. Fire would be sure to keep away from such a mixture if it were possible to do so.

The Fire Brigade of Paris, in 1866, consisted of about twelve hundred men in ten companies with a captain and two lieutenants. There were one hundred and thirty stations, with one hundred and eighty engines. The arrangement for fires consists of these stations, so distributed that if a fire breaks out the means of extinction may be near and arrive at once.

Each station is generally composed of one corporal and two firemen, and it is found that they, with the assistance of the neighbors, can extinguish a fire almost at its outbreak. If the fire grows more serious, other engines are called. Each theatre has an engine and two firemen at every representation. The engines are worked by eight men, and throw a large half-inch stream from ninety to one hundred feet high. They are placed in a hand-cart on an alarm, and carried to fires. A water-cask on a cart, with one hundred gallons of water, is also taken to each fire. Another cart also follows, containing all necessary fire tools. The advantage of this system of one hundred and thirty stations against the twenty of London, can be seen and appreciated by every person acquainted with fires. The Parisian engines can be taken from the carts and carried into the upper stories if necessary.

And now let me sketch, in the form of a city order, my plan for a new Boston Fire Department.

The Boston Fire Department shall be composed of two separate fire brigades.

The first brigade shall be the present department, leaving out the Extinguisher Brigade. Every steam-engine shall be altered, so that steam may be thrown into buildings, where the flames have not burst from the doors, windows, or roofs.

The chief of the second brigade shall place in every building — which from their great dimensions, or from the danger of taking fire of their contents, or for the safety of those employed in them, or for the safety of those who may be called there for instruction, business, or pleasure, such as churches, chapels, schools, halls, hospitals, theatres, hotels, boarding-houses, rooms where large numbers of females are employed, stables, stores in which are sold hay, straw, hemp, jute, manilla grass, powder, dualine, or other similar substances, oils, distilled spirits, wooden ware, furniture, and in every other store or manufactory, which may be deemed by him or the police to be necessary for the protection of the city from fire, — one small engine, three buckets, and one axe, together with a card of directions, as follows: —

WHAT TO DO IN CASE OF FIRE.

If there is a fire on these premises, the men or women appointed for that purpose will instantly take the engine and play upon the fire the water placed for them by other persons in the building.

A few minutes of cool, earnest, well-directed work may save your building from destruction, or preserve life, or possibly prevent a great fire.

N. B. — Every person in the building should keep cool, and aid those engaged in putting out the fire or keep out of their way.

—— ——, *Chief of Second Brigade.*

The expense of the Fire Plant shall be assessed on the owner or occupants of the building.

He shall also place in the dwellings, workshops, or stores of such places as the police report occupied by reliable men, at the expense of the city, small engines so near each other that one of them shall be within one minute of every building, in every thickly settled portion of the city. The engines shall be kept as near as possible in the same place in each building. If a fire not on the premises is put out by one of them before a steam-engine has thrown water upon it, the keeper shall be paid five dollars from the city.

Over a door of every building where an engine is kept a plate with the letters B. F. D., shall be placed.

A card with the following directions shall be hung near each engine : —

When called to a fire, take or send the engine instantly to it, and play the water already there upon the fire. Recollect that the earnest, well-directed work of a few minutes, may save your building, or may prevent a great fire.

If you put out a fire in any place except your own, before the steamer gets to work, you will be paid five dollars. When you have done working the engine, clean and hang it up to be ready for another call. If it is not in order report to the police.

———— ————, *Chief of the Second Brigade.*

There shall be placed in every house, shop, or store, where there is not an engine, the following card : —

BOSTON FIRE DEPARTMENT.

If your building is on fire send for the small engine at —— and fill your tubs and pails with water, and take them near the fire to be ready for use. Send also the alarm to the nearest telegraph box. Do not remove your furniture, as the fire will be out in a few minutes and make it unnecessary.

Keep this card hung up where it may be seen, and call the attention of the inmates to it.

—— ——, *Chief of the Second Brigade.*

Such a fire preventive and fire-fighting department should be placed in every city and large town in the United States. Where the Holly or other water-pressure system is in use, it would only be necessary to add the small engines for instant service. The hook and ladder companies may remain as at present, but with a premium of one thousand dollars for a ladder convenient, cheap, and safe, which should be so great an improvement as to cause its introduction by the city.

The cost of the Boston Fire Department for 1872 was $399,249. The cost of the three thousand engines, chief and assistants, with cards and all expenses, would be less than $50,000. That is, the whole second brigade the first year, purchasing all new engines, etc., would cost less than the land

and house of one steam-engine, and working it one
year! The power of the twenty-one steam fire-
engines is ten thousand five hundred gallons of
water per minute; of the four thousand engines;
twenty-four thousand gallons per minute. The
succeeding years the light brigade would cost perhaps fifteen thousand. But even this is not all
there is in favor of the new system. Almost all of
our fires would be put out without an alarm, and'
there would be few or no more conflagrations.

Now as a very great proportion of the firemen
work out of the department, and could be employed all the time at full pay, the city could reduce their salaries one half, quite to their advantage, and to that also of their other employers, and
that of the men as well. A saving of forty thousand dollars per annum could be made in this way.
Then the saving from the present wear and tear
of engines, horses, etc., would be more than the
annual expense of the second brigade after the
first year. But the financial advantage which
would be felt most would be that of insurance.
The rate of insurance would not be more than one
half of the present, while the insurers would be better paid than at present. Millions of dollars would
be saved every year to the citizens of Boston.

There are two doubts which may arise in some
minds and which I propose to examine.

The first is, Are the small engines really so efficient? I answer this question in the affirmative, and ask that a competent committee be appointed to make the proper investigations and experiments. All civilized nations do this when proving the best munitions of war, and surely this war of fire has become serious enough for us to wish to employ the best weapons against it.

The second doubt is, Would the small engines be worked efficiently? Would not those who have them be confused, excited, or terror-stricken, as people now are? Ask an army without weapons to stand up against one pouring showers of bullets, grape, and shell into them! Would not they run away in terror. The people near a fire have now no means of offense against it. Put them into their hands and they will at once go to work.

Every one of the four thousand men will become firemen; and working firemen too, at the very time and place where fire is most easily and successfully arrested.

The buildings assessed for the engines would be so much better protected that they would suffer no loss. And as the buildings which are more unsafe than others may also set fire to those near them, they should keep this protection for the general safety of a city.

There can be no doubt whatever, that if, such a

fire department as is here described had been in working order the night of the Chicago fire there would only have been burned Mrs. O'Leary's barn and contents. The showers of sparks which flew upon and set the half a dozen next buildings on fire, would have been dashed out, and any further danger prevented. But would the foreign population have known enough to use the engines. Use them?

At Chicago the foreign population kept the fire from crossing Jefferson Street, and saved their own property and millions of that remaining there to-day. If they could do that with buckets, they could have done ten times more with pails and small engines. Not a dollar's worth of property, except, perhaps, Mrs. O'Leary's barn, would have been lost, if there had been a system of large and small engines; the sparks would have been drowned out the moment they lit upon the roofs of the small buildings near it. The fire on Summer Street would hardly have warmed the Mansard roof on Otis Street before little streams from small engines would have been throwing water out upon it from its windows. Every spark which fell upon so many buildings at Portland, and set so many fires in that gale of wind, would have been drowned the second it lighted, and the only loss to that city would have been, perhaps, three hundred dollars.

And the next half dozen dreadful conflagrations, which are sure to occur sooner or later with the present ridiculous system, may be averted by a cheaper system, and the dreadful sufferings of many houseless people prevented.

MR. DAMRELL ON SMALL ENGINES AND EXTINGUISHERS.

On page 620 of the " Report of the Commissioners on the Cause and Management of the Great Fire in Boston," Mr. Damrell gives his objections to the use of Mr. Bird's idea of small engines, and tells why and how he uses the extinguishers.

Question.   " What do you think of these little hand-pumps ? "

Mr. Damrell.   "I think in some instances they serve very well.   But you must have a bucket of water with you.   You have got to carry a bucket of water in your hand.   We have them in the department ; we carry one on each carriage now — Mr. Bird's pumps."

Question.   " I understand that they are a part of the London equipment, and are very well spoken of ? "

Mr. Damrell.   " Yes, sir.   I use, instead of them now, the Babcock Fire Extinguisher, and have three companies organized.   They run to every fire.   There are two men who make that a specialty. They take the extinguishers and start, and in ten seconds can get up a pressure of sixty pounds to the square inch, which will throw a stream forty feet by the power of its own effervescence; consequently we find that they are much more effectual than the hand-pumps, where you have to carry a bucket of water, as it only throws a small stream. In the case of the extinguisher, you have only got to hold it: the power is behind it; it is automatic."

In these few lines he discards the pumps, approves the extinguishers, and describes the manner of using each kind. "We have them in the department." "We carry one on each carriage now." Does Mr. Damrell carry one in his carriage? Is one carried on either of the steam fire-engines? Is one taken to the fire on the hook and ladder carriage? or on the hose-carriage? I venture to say they are not carried on either one of them. If they were, as there are only three extinguisher wagons for the whole city, and as there are twenty-one steamers, ten hose-carriages, and seven hook-and-ladder companies, the small engines would put out nine out of ten of the fires which the extinguishers now do before these last arrived at the fire.

But "you have to carry a bucket of water in your hand." This tremendous objection is

stated three times. It possesses Mr. Damrell like
a nightmare. Just imagine Mr. Bird, with his
poor sciatic leg, standing at the head of State
Street with a bucket of water in one hand and a
little engine in the other, and see him, when the
telegraph strikes an alarm, starting off with all his
might, hippity, hoppity, almost two miles an hour,
for a fire which may be one or five miles away!
No, Mr. Damrell, Mr. Bird would do no such
thing; but it would be a far better method than
that you have taken of using extinguishers.   Mr.
Damrell has described his manner of using them,
and I venture to say that, under his introduction,
they have never put out a fire.   Certainly no such
fact has ever found a place in the newspapers of
the day.   I have described also my method of
using them.   Let the people judge between us.
Mr. Damrell takes on his coal or other carriages
perhaps half a dozen little pumps, and never uses
them, and calls that protecting the city with them.
Mr. Bird places at least four thousand of them,
each capable of dashing out a fire equal to that
of from six to ten tar or resin barrels well on fire,
or from twenty-four to forty thousand of them in
four thousand different places in a minute.   I pro-
test against his manner of introducing my engines.
I say it is not a practical, common-sense way.   I
say it is killing off an excellent idea by a mons-

trous, foolish way of putting it into practice. And I say also that Mr. Damrell's protection of the city of Boston — that is, the putting out of its small fires with three wagon-loads of extinguishers, and his tremendous manner of using the small engines, so well spoken of in Europe and this country — shows that he is willing to sacrifice the safety of the city to the show of teams rushing through the streets long after the time when four fifths of the fires would have been put out by the method described in this book for the use of small engines.

SMALL ENGINES FOR MANSARD ROOFS.

"So Naaman came with his horses and with his chariot, and stood at the door of the house of Elisha. And Elisha sent a messenger unto him, saying Go, and wash in Jordan seven times, and thy flesh shall come again to thee, and thou shalt be clean. But Naaman was wroth, and went away, and said, Behold, I thought, He will surely come out to me, and stand, and call on the name of the Lord his God, and strike his hand over the place, and recover the leper. Are not Abana and Pharpar, rivers of Damascus, better than all the waters of Israel? may I not wash in them, and be clean? So he turned and went away in a rage. And his servants came near, and spake unto him, and said, My father, if the prophet had bid thee do some great thing, wouldst thou not have done it? how much rather then, when he saith to thee, Wash, and be clean? Then went he down, and dipped himself seven times in Jordan, according to the saying of the man of God: and his flesh came again like unto the flesh of a little child, and he was clean." 2 KINGS v. 9–15.

The various plans proposed for extinguishing fires since the Boston conflagration, have so far failed entirely as regards the protection of the whole city, as they have been too expensive.   The poorer portion of the city will never be protected by them, and yet just there is where most of the conflagrations will be almost sure to commence.

Many years ago Professor Peirce was so kind as to examine into the efficiency of small engines used at once, as compared with the large ones when they could arrive ; and he said the advantage was immensely in favor of the small ones.   He offered to be one of one hundred to purchase them for the protection of Cambridge.   But those engines would have only gone into the houses of people who were careful and whose buildings were isolated.   The city, the crowded, dangerous portion of it would not have been protected.   That the small engines will put out fires, up to the size of ten or more tar-barrels, has been, and can be proved at any time; but how could they have been of any use, away up on a Mansard roof which could not be reached by the powerful steam-fire engines ?   In 1830, John Braithwaite of London, when his splendid new steam-fire engine was at work upon Barclay's Brewery which was on fire, and was destroyed, saved the malt-house and three hundred thousand dollars worth of malt in the following manner: " The beams on one side of the malt lofts had caught fire ; he went across one of the beams with two pint pots, carrying a gallon of water under his arm, and by applying it on the burning part, he extinguished the fire in the beams and the malt was saved." "Light blows kill the devil."

I wish to call particular attention to the following' assertion. With any good hand-engine and eight or ten feet of hose on the roof of the building, which first caught fire on its Mansard roof from the first store on fire, to play from it, back upon its own roof, it would not have taken fire ; and with half a dozen of them in the stores next to the first store on fire, only that one would have been burned, and the conflagration so disastrous to Boston would have been prevented.

There is not a Mansard roof in Boston from which a little stream directed from it back upon it, is not a sure protection against any danger from such a fire as was that of the first store burned in the great conflagration. The fire was kept from Hovey's store without them, but it was at the risk of life that a man went out as it were into the fire upon the slippery roof and saved it. The little engine would have, while its pipe was directed out and backwards, been vastly better, and the man who held it perfectly safe.

The Princess Theatre was on fire. A piece of blazing wood flew over another building and fell into a leaden gutter. The lead was melted and fell into the building into some oil on a work-bench, which it set on fire. It was seen and instantly put out. In five minutes there would have been another great fire, but fortunately a workman saw the accident in time to avert its consequences.

A great United States bonded warehouse is entered by the watchman at nine o'clock P. M. There is a little fire in some loose cotton away at the other end of the store, a hundred feet from the door. He is to watch against fire, but there is not even a pail or a dipper. With a pail of water and a London or Johnson pump he could have the fire out in a minute. He shuts the door and calls the Fire Department. Loss $600,000.

And we laugh at the folly of the people of Constantinople!

CHAPTER VI.

OUR DWELLING-HOUSES.

NOT long since I was in a splendid modern-built house in one of the cities near Boston. From cellar to attic I was shown how nice, cozy, convenient, elegant, grand, and rich were the different portions of this house, which had been built with the plans of an architect by first-rate carpenters, masons, plumbers, and painters, and filled with the fashionable furniture of the present day, with books, music, and everything which could gratify the most fastidious taste. It had all the modern improvements. And such houses are springing up in all our great towns and cities of our country, — every one " with all the modern improvements ; " and among those modern improvements there is not one dollar expended to prevent the destruction of these splendid buildings by fire. If the ever-present element of fire — in charge often of the most careless domestics, or from the furnace, fire-place, or stove, the lamp, gas, pipe, match, or cigar — once gets at work and finds its way into the ceiling or partition or stairway, there is room for it to play "hide-and-go-seek" from kitchen to parlor, from cellar to attic, in spite of the shrieks of the family and neighbors, and the yells of the populace, or the earnest, hard work of the fire department, when they arrive too late to be of any service. We then read: "The elegant mansion of —— took fire last night, and in spite of the most heroic efforts of the firemen, was totally destroyed. Every effort was made by those who first saw the fire to extinguish it, but it had burned its way through into the ceiling (partition or stairway, as the case may be), where it could not be reached, and the smoke soon drove those who were so earnestly engaged out of the house. The loss could not be less than (anywhere from twenty to one hundred thousand dollars). We most sincerely sympathize," etc.; but not one word of wisdom or caution as to the manner of building, or procuring means to prevent the destruction of another when by carelessness or accident it once takes fire.

One thousand dollars expended on that house in filling its partitions, ceilings, and stairways with material which would not burn, and a mere pittance for an axe, buckets, and a couple of pumps, would have saved that house, and would save ninety-nine of every hundred of such buildings from destruction when they take fire, if people would be wise enough to procure them.

FIRE-PROOF DWELLING-HOUSES.

There can be little or no doubt that, with a proper amount of attention to the subject, and a liberal amount of money to commence with, there could be dwellings erected of concrete, cheaper, more durable, warmer in cold, cooler in warm weather, and absolutely fire-proof. Many such are now erected in England, Austria, and other portions of Europe, and a few in this country. A little of the money we may be called upon for charity, to save from starvation the population of a city destroyed by fire, would bring into use houses which could not be destroyed. Here and there are a few in this country, but some of them are badly made, and some of the material does not " stand the weather," and they crumble with the frost.

At Vienna, concrete houses are covered with terra-cotta, which preserves them for centuries.

The time will soon come when timber and wood will be too dear for poor people to use. The awful waste of it by fire will soon make it as scarce as it is at Paris. Then Yankee ingenuity will invent dwellings in which there will be no wood, inside or outside! Then a man's house will indeed be his castle, his place of shelter, his ark of safety.

Would that Massachusetts in her wisdom could

see that it would be for her interest to offer premiums for this purpose, so liberal as to insure this great blessing at once to all within her limits. Premiums for horses, mares, colts, bulls, cows, calves, hogs, pigs, sheep, and goats; premiums for apples, pears, plums, peaches, corn, wheat, rye, pumpkins, and squashes; aye, for thousands of other things, all good and proper, and yet all combined are not as important as that the people should live in good, healthy houses, wholly indestructible by fire. I believe it would make people more careful and more provident if they could realize that, once owning a house, it would always be their own, and not subject to the risk of being destroyed at any hour. Fifty thousand dollars given for premiums for this purpose would save millions of dollars worth of the firesides of the people, and the feeling of security would be of more value than untold millions.

A LETTER FROM THE SCULPTOR POWERS.

There appeared lately in the " Providence Journal," a letter from the sculptor, Mr. Hiram Powers, which I regard as an important testimony on this point, and I give it entire.

FLORENCE, *December* 2, 1871.

MY DEAR SIR:— Your letter recalls to my mind what I have more than once said to my countrymen, namely,

That the day was not distant when one or more of our American cities would be destroyed by fire. I made this prediction to you, I remember, and I am sorry, indeed, that it has been so soon fulfilled. It only requires a combination of circumstances similar to those which existed at Chicago, to lay in ashes any other American city. Let the cold be below zero, with a tempestuous wind and the hour the dead of the night, when all are at rest, and a fire begin in some huge block of buildings full of combustibles, petroleum, etc., and just in the spot to be taken by the wind and swept through the city, and there will be another Chicago disaster. It is true that Chicago was built for a bonfire. Even the roofs were of pitch, I have been told. It was the strong wind, however, which did the business, and will do it again with a combustible city. And I fear that there is not in America a city which is not combustible. There may be some fire-proof buildings, but more depends upon their isolation than their structure. The fire at Chicago swept away fire-proofs and all in its way.

But it may be asked, " Is it possible to make a city fire-proof?" I answer, yes ; and without any great extra expense. To prove this, I have only to say that although there have been frequent fires in the city of Florence during the thirty-four years of my residence in it, not one house has been consumed, except a theatre, and that was not entirely destroyed. Rooms, full of goods, have been heated like ovens by ignited calicoes, straw hats, etc., but as the floors above and below were all covered by thin brick tiles, the goods burned *without ventilation.* And as there was no flame, a smell like that of a coal-pit soon gave the alarm, and the fire was soon extinguished by no other engine than a squirt holding about a gallon, which discharged a well-directed stream through some aperture. I once beheld some firemen marching to a fire in Florence. Foremost were three men with picks, next four men with buckets, then three men with highly polished brass squirts on their shoulders; all marching with an air of pomp and importance. The fire was at the residence of Mr. Clevenger, the American sculptor, and had been burning twenty-four hours on the end of a joist just under his fireplace. He had smelt something like a coal-pit for some time, and at length perceived smoke rising from the brick floor. On going below he found the room full of smoke, and a rush-bottomed chair just under the joist was partially consumed. But the joist was not yet burned off, and why? Because the fire was *bricked down.* It could not rise and burst into flames.

The secret of fire-proof building then, is this : It must be made impossible for the flames to pass through the floors or up the stairway. If you will have wood floors and stairs, lay a flooring of the thinnest sheet-iron over the joists, and your wood upon that ; and sheath the stairs with the same material. A floor will not burn without a supply of air under it. Throw a dry board upon a perfectly flat pavement and kindle it as it lies if you can. You may make a fire upon it and in time consume it, but it will require a long time. Prevent drafts, and though there will still be fires, no house will be consumed. The combustion will go on so slowly that discovery is certain in time to prevent any great calamity. But the roofs, the roofs, how about them? Slate or tiles. Zinc melts too easily. I believe that hard burned tiles, if flat, would stand the frost at home; and if so they constitute the best roofing. My house *has no joists.* All the floors are of tiles resting on arches. One of these arches was made over a room twenty-five feet square, by four men in four days. The bricks are about one and one half inches thick, and laid *edgewise*, with plaster of Paris. There was no framework prepared to lay them on, unless you would so term four bits of wood which a man could carry under his arm. And yet this arch is so strong as to be perfectly safe with a large dancing-party on it. I never have heard of one of those floors falling, and they are absolutely fire-proof. Of course, light arches like these would not do for warehouses. It would pay, I think, to send out here for an Italian brick-mason who knows how to build these thin but strong arches for dwelling-houses. I know that there is a prejudice at home against brick or composition floors. "Too cold in winter," it is said. And so they are if bare, but cover them with several thicknesses of paper and then carpet them, and no one can distinguish the slightest difference between their temperature and that of wood floors. Who doubts this let him try the experiment with the feet or the thermometer. The truth is that the brick or composition floor is no colder *in itself* than wood — the thermometer attests this, — but it is a better conductor.

I do not insure my house as I know that it is not combustible.   Yours, truly,

                              HIRAM POWERS.

But until the good time comes when our houses
shall be fire-proof — let us consider the common
causes of fire in our dwellings, and first,

THE DANGER OF FIRE FROM STOVES.

Most people suppose the principal danger from
the use of stoves is from defective flues. A funnel is inserted into the chimney, through the partitions, in the cheapest and most careless possible
manner, and watched for a few days to see if it
takes fire. If it does not, it is pronounced "perfectly safe." Now the wood which it almost
touches may have just been cut from the forest,
and is as wet as a soaked sponge, and would hardly
take fire if put in a furnace. But in one, three, or
five years, the stove fires have made it as dry as
tinder, and then the red-hot funnel converts it
to charcoal, and the next time the funnel heats it
to two hundred and twelve, it takes fire from
spontaneous combustion. Then if the family have
read this book, they will extinguish the fire with
their little " Fire Brigade," with a loss of only a
few dollars, but if not, in the confusion and the
terror of the fire and smoke, and with nothing to

work with, the fire will run through, and destroy the house in about an hour.

But another danger is where stoves are set, not on the brick hearth, but in any part of a room, on the wood floor, with only a plate of zinc, iron, or tin between them. Mr. Braidwood says, " In a fire at the Bank of England, the hearth on which the stove was placed was cast iron an inch thick, with two and a half inches of concrete underneath it ; but the timber below it was fired." The heat from the stove in a few years makes charcoal of the wooden floor under the zinc or iron plate, when it takes fire at two hundred and twelve, and the plate above prevents the fire rising upwards, so it burns through to the space between the floors, and then up, to all parts of the house, store, or warehouse. If the fire breaks out in the daytime there is an alarm, when the steamers pour in their water, and the loss by fire and water is hundreds or perhaps thousands of dollars. If it breaks out in the night the building is destroyed with its contents, and if in a gale of wind there is a destructive fire or a conflagration. There are thousands of stoves in our cities and towns, under which this manufacture of charcoal is busily going on, and where a fire may take place, any day or night. No stove should be set except on a good brick hearth which should be laid on sand, or some other non-fire conductor.

Fires are continually discovered where no direct agency can be found, and where they burst out so far from the stove that no one suspects it, and yet they are from that cause alone. Insurance offices should refuse to take a risk on any property in which a stove is used, which is not set on a brick hearth. It should also be the duty of inspectors of buildings to place such hearths under all stoves which are used without them at the expense of the occupants of the buildings. This may seem to the occupants to be severe, but the safety of cities and large towns require that means shall be applied, both for preventing and for fighting fires which may make them more safe than at present. And if proper means of prevention are applied, we may be certain that the rate of insurance will fall so as to more than meet any expense we may incur by doing it.

OF DANGER FROM FURNACES.

If the property which has been consumed by fires from furnaces in Massachusetts could be footed up in one sum it would astonish even those who are best acquainted with the subject. Churches, halls, town and city halls, schools, and dwelling-houses, have all suffered from this prolific cause of fire, which has been reported as "defective furnace." Years past this was true.

A gentleman who had erected a number of dwell-ing-houses, after three had been burned, took out the rest and had others put in their places. There were no more fires. But if we now wish a fur-nace, and will give the workmen room enough, there will be very little danger from fire from it. But a church is to be erected. A committee of popular members is chosen to direct the matter, but who know nothing of building in general, or of furnaces in particular. The house is to be —— by ——, and is to contain the great room, for Sun-day service, a great and a small vestry, and as many other rooms as the oft quoted old lady, who had a " great box, little box, bandbox, and bundle," besides a kitchen large enough for a hotel, so that the furnace, which most of all should have all pos-sible room, is crowded into the smallest possible space. The first year all is safe, and perhaps the second, and the committee laugh at the fools who told of danger. At last there comes a cold Sun-day. The congregation are almost frozen in the morning service, and as they go out they each one have a cross word at the sexton. Before they have all " piled it on him," he is the most irate man in town, and runs to inflict his anger on the poor fire. How he makes it burn! Then the wind rises and the furnace gets hotter. In the afternoon the house is hotter, and in the evening the windows

must be opened, and before morning the splendid
church is a heap of ruins. The same story will
apply to nine tenths of all other fires which have
been occasioned by furnaces, so crowded that the
wood touched, or was too near the heated flues,
or too near the fire. Room! should be the cry
of the mason who is to set it. Try to purchase
the best furnace there is, give it all the room
it wants, and then see the workmen set it, that
you may know where is the place of greatest danger.

If a fire takes from a furnace the fire department should be notified as soon as possible. In the
mean time, if you have a small engine, put it to
work, and with an axe and plenty of water you
may be able to get at the place of danger, and
have the fire out before they arrive. Never cut a
hole into where there is fire until you have water
to throw upon the fire. But the best way to fight
a furnace fire is by prevention. " An ounce of
prevention is better than a pound of cure." Take
a pound of prevention in room, and insist upon·
a careful setting of your furnace by skillful workmen. Then learn how to manage it, and never
heat it to its fullest extent; and recollect that
by using it carefully it will last a long time, and
all that time it will be safe, or as safe as anything can be, where so much heat must be near

wood. We shall never have perfect safety until we make houses almost entirely of concrete or brick. Let us hope that time will soon come.

OF MATCHES.

"Matches are made in heaven," but not friction matches. It has long been the world's wonder where all the pins go to. But I think that in this country more matches are lost than pins. I have sometimes, at a fire, required a light (for you see a man with a little engine soon dashes out the light of a fire), and I have been surprised to see every boy clap his hand to his vest pocket to hand me one. We all know how easy it is to lose a knife, but for every knife lost, a gross of matches are dropped in the wood-shop, among the chips and shavings; in the barn, among the hay and straw; in the rooms, to be swept up and put away in the clutter-box, or in some other way get into places where they may set fire. Many a man whose property has happened to be well insured has been suspected of setting fire to his buildings, when they have gone off from the agency of a lost friction match. There were a thousand chances that a mouse or a rat, or one of the five cows, or the horse in Mrs. O'Leary's barn, set with a match the fire which burned Chicago, than that she or any one else was milking a cow who kicked over a lamp.

Rats and mice like phosphorus, and they will try to get the little of it which is on almost every friction match. It is not every one which burns its nose that sets a fire. If it did we should be sadly off. But a gentleman not long since, while standing near a little heap of rubbish, heard a mouse cry out as if in pain. He saw him rush out of the heap, and as he crossed the floor a tiny sneeze or two attracted his attention. Looking back at the rubbish he saw a little smoke rising from it, and he at once went to work to unravel the mystery. Carefully opening the heap he came to a burning match which had already set fire to the heap. Now the mystery was solved. The mouse found the match and went for the phosphorus ; the match took fire, which burnt his nose, when his squeal, and the cough and sneeze, called the man to the · danger, and he was able to save his house without a little engine.

A FEW WORDS TO AMERICAN WOMEN.

By far the keenest suffering which is felt from the fires of our dwellings or other property falls upon the gentler sex. The man " roughs it," and braves it with bold, strong words, but it sinks into the heart of the female sex to be driven from her home in such a fearful, frightful manner. Then, with the new home I fear more care will be expended in that which is for the man than for the woman. It is a shame, but, alas, I fear it is only too true. The man knows much better what he needs for his comfort than he does of the necessities of his helpmeet, and so when the money is expended it is too much, far too much, for his convenience, and too little for the comfort of his " better half." For this I shall not advise you to hold indignation meetings, or to insist upon the right of suffrage, though I think that would be an immense blessing to the male portion of creation. I only propose to offer you a few words of advice upon a subject to which I have given much attention, and to which most of you have given very little, that of the best manner of extinguishing fires in the house, if you should be so unfortunate as to have one there. You are much more at home than we of the stronger sex, and it is at the first instant of the discovery of a fire that it can best be put out. A pail or two, a dipper or two, and an axe or a hatchet, well used, will, four times out of five, put out the fires that occur in or about a house in a few minutes. Do not be frightened when you are told of a fire on your premises. It can do no good, and may do much harm. Is it in a chamber? Do not open the door until you have ready one or two pails of water and a dipper. Call for help, but go to work yourself. You will feel much better than if you keep still and see your house burning up. A lady in Milton made up a fire in an open fire-place in an upper room, where children slept in the night. Returning soon after to the room she found it in flames. Carefully pouring upon it the water of the pitcher first, she found a pail of water and another pitcher full, and with them she succeeded in quelling the fire. The quilt, comforter, four blankets, flounce, feather bed, and mattress were well burned before she arrested it. The smoke from all this must have quite filled the room, and I fear most of you would have cried for help or given the alarm, when the house would have been destroyed. The lady put out the fire without giving an alarm to the inmates of the house. While I commend her for her self-possession, I think it would have been more safe to have called them up. Mr. Braidwood never allows a man to enter a house alone which is on fire. I have no doubt, however, she measured the work to do, saw she could do it, and then went about it and finished it. All honor to her, and may her example be followed by all females (and males, if they dare to) who find such fires at work in their homes. A smoke arising from the cellar is much more dangerous than from a room up-stairs. If it is dense you had better not risk your life without help, if it is at hand.

Fires in the ceiling, partitions, in the stairway: first have your water and dipper ready, then break a hole with an axe, through to it, and throw the water with all your force, from the dipper, upon it. You may have to make several holes, but if you work with energy you will soon have it all out. It will be better to exert yourself very much indeed, saving your home, than to lose it. And here let me ask you to purchase for this purpose a Johnson pump. It is so light, so easy to handle, and a woman can work it so nicely, and it is so efficient that no family should be without one. The Milton lady could have put out ten times more fire with one of them than she could without it. Then the water can be thrown by women to the roofs of most houses.

But I wish to tell of a fire at Athol, Mass., and of an excellent rule of a family there. A fire was built in an air-tight stove, and a basket of chips, left too near, took fire. When discovered, the wooden mantel was on fire, and the carpet and floor; and the flames had risen to the ceiling. The lady who saw it went through two rooms, took a pail of water and a dipper, returned with them, and put out the fire. The rule was that there should always be a pail full of water ready in the house. It was ready, and the house was saved. I have given directions in another place for you if your clothes take fire. Will you do me the favor to read them. If "fire is found on the roof, and you have a pump, you can easily put it out if your house is not too high. The pump is worth its cost for cleaning windows. But it gives a feeling of safety, which is of much more value than its expense; and the having it will call your attention to the subject, and you will think of what you should do if you were in danger from fire. The following anecdote of a great fire will, I think, be of use to persons living in villages: —

A great manufactory, some distance from a village, was in flames; the wind was blowing the sparks and pieces of burning wood over the entire village, which consisted almost entirely of wooden buildings. The men were all off to the fire, and the fire was catching on every house. The women were equal to the occasion, and every fire was climbed to and dashed out before it could do any harm. No doubt they ran some risk; but what a pleasure it must have been, what a comfort, that their beautiful village, the home of a thousand people, was not in ruins, as was the great manufactory, the cause of the danger. In another place I have related how well a woman mopped out a fire, and do not forget that the best managed fire I ever saw was directed by one. It is much more pleasant to fight a fire with all your might, even if you lose your house, than to stand weeping while it is burning, while the chances are twenty to one that you will save it. It is not fair to have the stories all on one side, therefore here is one of caution. A woman, having a pot of grease, for some strange reason placed it in the stove. Soon it was time for tea, and the fire was started. A great puff of smoke, a flash of flame, and open burst the stove doors, to show the pot of grease about to make a monstrous grease-spot! Her son, however, a bright boy, caught it, and it was out of the window in a twinkling. The house was saved from almost certain destruction, but the hands of the boy were badly burned by his brilliant exploit, as it would be termed if telling a story of a battle. ·

I do not suppose any lady ever wears jute about her head; but will you be so good as to say to your servant that it is very dangerous. Too often do women lose their lives by this means. It is, however, so much more respectable to say that a person was burned to death by her clothes taking fire, than that her head was burnt off by the jute taking fire, that we seldom hear of such a "shocking catastrophe!"

Sometimes the clothes on a clothes-horse take fire. Throw it flat on the floor, if possible. In all such cases take care that your own clothes do not take fire, as this is a greater danger than all others. When children are on fire, if they run at you, be careful, or you may also be enveloped in flames. If by running away from them a few steps you can grasp a rug, shawl, overcoat, or any other woolen cloth, you had better do so, as it will be more safe for you and the sufferer also. Of course, if the fire is not large, you can manage it; yet even then, if your hands are not covered with a woolen cloth, they may be burned so as to give you much pain. If in the night you find the house on fire and full of smoke, and cannot go down the stairs, tie the ends of two sheets together, and come down on the outside as fast as possible. I think that families in the country should as much as possible avoid sleeping above the second story. There is no great danger at that height, but one other adds greatly to it.

But there are other points than the safety of life and from fire in the house which ladies may understand and defend from the attack of fire. Seldom have I received such pleasure as one day the past winter at the mansion of one of the princely merchants of Boston. A daughter, who had looked into the subject since the great fire, described the dangerous places on the outside of the house where sparks could light, and light the house into a new fire. Then she described how she could reach and extinguish them with an engine. How I wished she and a company of her female friends could have been at Otis Street at the November fire. About $80,000,000 would have been saved by them in an hour! It may seem a service rather unfit for young women to fight fires; but if the men fail, as at that fire, and the women, by their tact and ready wit, can be so efficient, we should be thankful for their assistance. They can at least teach the men to adopt a system so efficient, and that will perhaps be the work they can do best at the present time. " If they will, they will, you may depend on't ! " I hope they will.

CHAPTER VII.

TURNING now from private dwellings to stores and public buildings, let us consider, first, elevators, and then what I call fire elevators, or chip and shaving hatchways.

ELEVATORS.

One of the common items of city news, is that of loss of life, or maimed for life, by people in warehouses falling down elevator passages. It is one prolific source of the practice of our hospitals. When such an accident occurs, those who see the broken, crushed mass of humanity carried off to the hospital or its home, are dreadfully shocked. A few of them may possibly dare whisper that the man-trap should not forever be set, to murder, or worse, to cause the unfortunate person to linger on, a poor crippled man, forever dependent on the help of his friends, often little able to support him. But the " package " is removed, and the business of the merchant goes on just as before. The trap continues set, because it would cost **a** few hundred dollars to make a proper elevator, which may be wanted for the purchase of the next horse or carriage, with which to ride upon the fashionable drives about the city.

Another item which helps to fill the newspapers, is somewhat as follows : " Destructive Fire. The warehouse of ——, was found on fire last night by persons passing on the street. There seemed to be but little fire, and that in the basement. It soon however ran up the elevator, and although the fire department was on hand as usual, yet before they got to work the flames had broken out in every loft, and the merchandise was all in flames. The department succeeded in confining the fire to one store, but the loss in that was very large, probably some hundred thousands." This would be varied, not exactly according to the weather, but of the wind, so as to embrace several stores, or a street, or as on the November fire would become an awful conflagration, involving dreadful loss of life and misery untold upon thousands of people. Why then do not the merchants provide themselves with safety elevators, which can never be open except when packages are passing through them ? Because it is not the law, with a severe penalty, that they shall be placed in every store, warehouse, etc. That is the simple reason. It costs something. One man may have in his place of business such a proper safeguard from awful accident, to life, or from the destruction of the city, and the papers may call attention to it, and they are always willing to do their full share of such good works, and thousands of owners and people renting stores shall see them, and not half a dozen of them will be put up in a year, and the inventor will grow poor after inventing what if brought into use as it should be, would render life and property much more safe. It is a good time now to make such a law. Those who have not been burned out can well afford to meet the expense, and where new buildings are to be erected the extra expense is but trifling. Our papers constantly contain advertisments with minute descriptions of safety elevators. The inventors should for the next few months be overrun with orders; yet if there is no law enacted they will sell about a dozen in the city, during the year, when it should not close without there being many thousands of them brought into use.

An excellent safety elevator which was patented in 1856 by W. H. Thompson and E. P. Morgan, had sold up to 1870, only sixty-five of them, and almost every one of them were placed in manufactories. There should be sixty-five hundred of them in Boston. For the safety of the city, and a protection against fire, they are required. For the safety of the firemen, who often have to grope their way through buildings filled with smoke to extinguish fires, they are required.   For the prevention of cruelty to animals, as man is an animal, for how often do we read of a merchant, or his customer, his clerk, boy, or one of the porters, falling from one to half a dozen stories, to be carried off to a hospital a mangled creature, or to his home a corpse.   Does it cost a few hundred dollars? Not one.   The greater safety from fire will pay for them.   The pleasant feeling of security from accidents from their use would be worth thousands of dollars to every man who pulls out the old, and introduces a new safety elevator, safe from dreadful accidents, and from fires.   In spite of the dreadful mistake of those who failed to give an alarm to the telegraph for twenty minutes at the Boston fire, if there had been a safety elevator in the first store which took fire, the fire would most likely have never gone out of the basement, and the loss by the fire would have been less thousands than it was millions of dollars. There are laws against smoking, drinking, selling drinks, against taking a newspaper, loaf of bread, or a thousand other trivial items. Now let us make it a crime to set these man and fire traps all over the city, and by a severe penalty compel every person using an elevator to procure a safe one.

Of all the dangerous things about a city none are more to be dreaded than the open wood spaces through which the refuse wood is sent from each story to the basement, to be consumed by the fire which is to furnish motive power for the manufactory. They are chimneys of wood with openings at each story. Then, when a fire catches at the bottom, it rushes up the narrow space, roaring like a chimney on fire, and in a moment or two, often before an alarm can be sounded, the great building is on fire in every story, and before a steamer can be got to work the fire has enveloped the building and become so intense that even the steamers can be of little other use than to confine the fire to the first building. It is to be hoped that there are few of these dangerous places in any city, as so many great buildings have been destroyed by them, that it is found cheaper and safer to construct them of iron. The Mason and Hamlin reed organ factory, on Cambridge Street, was burned from varnish taking fire in the basement and running up the wooden chimney. If the fire had been kept in the basement by a sheet of iron, the first engine would have made short work of it; for want of that, it was in every story before it got to work at it. The great pianoforte manufactory, which was burned on the ground on which now stands the St. James Hotel, was first found to be on fire in the third or fourth story, having caught in the basement, and first seen up there, though it was at work in all the lower stories. There is not the smallest chance to put out such a fire. It is a monstrous battle between the element of fire and the combustible matter of the building, while the firemen attempt to prevent the fire from destroying other buildings. In a gale of wind the firemen often have to fight almost like demons to prevent the destruction of whole districts. I have no doubt that quite often it has required the most heroic and dangerous efforts of the firemen to preserve a city from dreadful conflagrations, when such great fire-traps have, in a few minutes, become monstrous fires. The most stringent laws should be enacted against all such traps made of wood, or even of iron, unless with doors which should shut off each room, and which should always be closed when not in use. I recollect a fire near the railroad bridge, on Tremont Street, in such a building, which, when first seen, was so small as to hardly have any flame. No means of putting out the fire less than a steamer was thought of or was at hand, and that half a mile away. Yet even when that arrived, it was for a few moments difficult to see any fire. This state of things, however, was of short duration. The fire was in the wooden " fire-elevator," and in a few moments the whole building was a mass of flames, which threatened many others. By the noble exertions of the firemen it was mainly confined to one great establishment, but the danger to a great portion of the city was imminent. There should be stringent laws against all such places, which might, in a gale of wind, do immense damage. But must we have laws for everything? Yes; against everything which may endanger a city or town. We have laws against shooting robins and sparrows, or breaking off a shrub or flower in the Public Garden. This is right; but a thousand times more proper would be laws against every kind of careless use or abuse of fire. Think of Chicago and Boston, and then say if this is not true.

I wish now to speak of common causes of fire in our buildings, and first of —

DANGER OF FIRE FROM RUBBISH IN CELLARS.

" *September* 10, 1666. All the morning clearing our cellars, and breaking in pieces all my old timber, to make room and *to prevent fire.*" — Pepy's *Diary.*

Every farm is said to have its clutter hole. I am afraid every house has one also, and I am sure that too many warehouses and stores have them in the cellar. The danger in cities from the old broken wood and paper-boxes, etc., is very great indeed, and especially when the cellars commu-

nicate with elevators, such as are in common
use, but which, by stringent laws, should be prevented.   Fire, when it catches upon bales of
woolen or cotton, or similar goods, in the basement of a store, burns very slow, but when it is
in a cord or two of dry boards and heaps of old
paper boxes, it soon creates a flame which destroys
the contents of the room, if luckily it does not
cause a dreadful conflagration.   There are a great
many places in every city and town, " up-stairs
and down-stairs," which, if the merchants would
" clean up," to make room and to prevent fire, the
communities would be all the safer for it.   Near
eight hundred such places were pretty effectually
cleared up one night and day last fall, but there
are many hundreds left which should be at once
attended to, that another desolating fire may not
occur.   In basements where goods are packed,
there should be especial care of fire.   Some years
since, on a windy day, I went into the basement
of a store, where there was a stove, in which was
a very hot fire, and the stove almost red hot.
Near it were piled up dozens of pails, packed in
straw, and the whole cellar was full of like combustible matter.   Knowing how easy it would be
for a cat or rat to overturn them, or the natural
tendency of such things to fall over, and the ab-
solute certainty of the destruction of the whole

store, if once on fire, and the danger to the city
in a gale of wind, I cautioned a young gentleman
of the danger. I was answered good-naturedly
that it was no matter, they were well insured, if
the old thing did go up. He was an excellent
young man, and would not do what he thought
wrong. But the same remark is quite too common,
and the carelessness to which it leads, I think, is
the cause of not a few of our basement and other
fires. Such a remark would be looked upon as
almost a crime in a respectable store in Liverpool or London, and it should never be made
anywhere.

SMOKING DURING BUSINESS HOURS.

There should be at once in every city and town
severe laws enacted against smoking in any building or street during business hours. Not only
many thousands, but millions of dollars worth of
property have been destroyed from this smoking
evil. It is said that fires cannot be set in this
manner; and so it is said that they cannot by oiled
rags, and the one is just as true as the other.
Only a few days since a pretty little fire was got
up in a railway car, set by a lighted pipe, thrust
into an Irishman's pocket. Some time since a
gentleman in Jamaica Plain passing his barn saw
smoke coming out of the door. Following it back

into the harness room he saw fire in a coat, and on taking it up to throw out of the barn, a pipe dropped from it, showing the cause of the fire.

Not a few of the fires for which no cause is found are of this origin. The great fire which commenced on Battery Wharf, July 27, 1855, was no doubt set by a workman who was smoking about the loose and drying cotton. The loss was five hundred thousand dollars.

The great fire at London in 1861, which destroyed eleven millions of dollars worth of merchandise, etc., was said to have originated from spontaneous combustion in hemp. But the chances were ten to one that the cause was a workman's pipe. The same cause may be assigned, I believe, for the fire in a cordage store which caused such a sensation a few years since in Boston. A gentleman who is in the hay and straw business told me, a few days since, that it was quite common, especially in wet weather, for people in the streets to come in to the hay stores, while passing, if they saw no one, and lighting a match and then their pipe, to throw the match down among the loose hay. He thought that almost all the hay fires were caused in that way. He said their own men were forbidden to smoke; but I believe some of their worst fires have been brought about by their own workmen smoking " on the sly." He also said that most of the hay fires occur in wet weather, the time when outsiders come in to light their pipes.

I once saw a most careless act of lighting a pipe. Several workmen came out from breakfast to the workshop, which was in a barn. One of them — and shame to him a Yankee — caught up a handful of shavings, lighted them with a match, then lighted his pipe with the shavings, and without looking at them crushed the shavings in his hand and threw them out of sight under the bench! There were cords of shavings about, and many tons of hay in the barn! But there was not a carpenter's workshop there another day! All over the country, fires are occurring from such causes, and it would be well to enact that if we are to have an eight or ten hour law, no portion of the time should be spent in setting fires by smoking pipes, or tobacco in any form.

STORE FIRE BRIGADE.

People are too much accustomed to leave to others what they could better do themselves. How many will read this little work, and then leave the whole question to be settled by the present fire department. So have the people gone on for years with the small-pox question, and would have still, perhaps, had not some facts come

to light which startled the public to action. So
should the fires of Chicago, Boston, and other
places awaken the business portion of all other
cities to look into the subject for themselves. A
Boston merchant writes to the " Advertiser " that
he is going to get up a store fire brigade. So have
they at Hovey's store, and also at a few others.
Every head of an establishment should select some
man and have him get up a little band of the
inmates, who would be engine-men, axe-men, or
water-carriers, with others to take their places if
wanted. The idea that this will tend to make
them worse book-keepers or salesmen is absurd.
Every man will become more a man if he can put
out a fire or do any other good thing for you.

HOTEL FIRE BRIGADE.

Many years ago there was a fire department in
the Burnet House, at Cincinnati. Every man had
some place assigned him, to which he instantly
hastened when the alarm bell struck. All hotels
should have hose always ready at a moment's
warning, with men to man it, and axe-men, fire
buckets, and small engines, with directions on
printed cards hung in every story, and men
trained to use them instantly, in case of an alarm
in the house. There would be very few lives lost
in hotels if these precautions were observed. The

men should feel that their own safety depended upon these " fire brigades," and that it was their duty — a part of their contract as workmen — to do what they could for the safety of the patrons of the house. The dreadful disaster at the hotel at Richmond, Virginia, some time since, would not have occurred with such a system, as it was seen when a few dashes of water upon the flames would have kept them back until the inmates could have escaped. With such a system, too, the " brigade " would have seen the dangerous condition of the women at the hotel in New York, and means would have been found to save them.

THE CHICKERING FIRE BRIGADE.

This fire brigade, in their great piano-forte warehouse on Tremont Street, is perhaps the best private fire preventive establishment in the United States, if not in the world.

Thirty fifty-feet lengths of hose are always attached to water-pipes and ready in a moment.

Forty-five extinguishers are so distributed that one may be at work in a minute. Axes, iron-bars, spanners, and other tools are distributed about the building.

One captain, ten lieutenants, and one hundred and fifty men, are trained to fly to their places at a cry of fire, or at the stroke of the fire-bell.

Double iron doors separate the wings from the main building in each story, and water keeps them wet and cool in case of fire.

The chips are taken from the rooms in great barrows, to the elevator, and thence to the floor, from whence they are wheeled to an iron room, and kept for use.

The lumber in the dry houses is safe, as the houses can be filled with steam in a few minutes. The watchmen are trained to use the extinguishers, etc., in case of fire in the night.

With their well-trained and intelligent workmen, their means of extinguishing fires, they set a most excellent example to all other business places in towns and cities.

The expense is of course great, but the Messrs. Chickering have no doubt it pays them for all the outlay. Three fires, one very dangerous, have already been extinguished. The sight of the fire tools and the drills of the firemen have no doubt prevented many others.

OF BUILDINGS WHICH ARE IN GREAT DANGER OF TAKING FIRE.

Of all the buildings exposed to fire none are in such constant danger as the manufactories of friction matches. Yet it is very seldom that one of them is destroyed. The reason is that, knowing the danger, and that the town or city departments could not get the alarm and get to work until their property was destroyed, they organize a fire brigade of their own. Some of them have extinguishers and some little pumps, and some of them both ; and yet most of the fires there are smothered out by a wet woolen cloth or a pint of water, without waiting for the larger machines.

I have known of foundries in the country, where, when there was a dry time, a workman was stationed outside to see if the roof did not take fire. Placing a ladder on the side of the building, and a bucket of water at the foot of the ladder, if a fire started he was a complete "fire brigade" in himself, and before the fire could spread a foot in diameter he dashed it out and filled his bucket for another battle, which, instead of being a defeat, as are almost all of our fires between the town and the city departments, always ended in a splendid victory. Now for the reason. The "bucket brigade" was right at the fire when it commenced, and the bucket contained water enough to drown out all the fire in an instant ; yet those same little fires, if neglected until the whole village could be notified, and the young men run to the engine, run it to the fire, get it to the water, if there was any, which often there is not, and then get it ready to play, would completely envelop and destroy the building, or perhaps a village.

MANSARD ROOFS.

From the history of the introduction of the beautiful structures now becoming so fashionable in this country, called Mansard-roof buildings, and from the different manner of building them in this country and that in Paris, two lessons may be learned by such persons as care to grow wise as they grow old. The first is the " masterly inactivity " which attends the dissemination of real improvements throughout the civilized world. Mansard, an architect of Paris, the builder of the celebrated Palace of the Tuileries and many other of the best structures in Paris, and who invented the elegant roof which bears his name, died in 1666, the year of the great fire of London. Yet they have only been known in this vicinity about twenty years, and it is not more than five years since a New York letter-writer boasted that a few of them were going up in that vicinity, though they were becoming common here. The second lesson is that the devil is almost sure to get his claws into any real improvement and so to arrange matters that more evil than good will attend its introduction. The Mansard-roofed buildings in Paris, from the wise manner of building in that

city, where as much stone, brick, iron, mortar, and
rubble, and as little wood as possible, is used, with
their wonderfully efficient fire brigade, make a safe
and elegant style of architecture.

The Mansard-roofed structures, as made in our
cities and villages, are the most dangerous buildings ever constructed, and if the fashion now so
prevalent of building them does not abate or
change, but they continue to increase for the next
five years, as they have for five years, they will
as assuredly cause the destruction of our cities, as
any other effect follows its cause, as sure as the
tide ebbs and flows, or the sun rises and sets. In
many places the law forbids the erection of wooden
buildings to more than a certain height — say
thirty or forty feet, — but these buildings are carried up from fifty to a hundred feet of wood, iron,
stone, and brick, on the top of which is placed a
wooden roof, covering from an eighth of an acre to
an acre of buildings, and from ten to thirty feet
high. Why, some of these immense structures
contain more boards, plank, joist, timbers, lath,
etc., than half a dozen country lumber-yards,
These monstrous buildings may seem beautiful to
the eye, and may add to the attraction of a city
when looked upon by those who do not know of
the danger which may attend their destruction by
fire ; but unless they can be built of some other

material than they are at present, unless the wood can be kyanized so that it will not burn, or iron substituted for wood, they should, at the next session of the legislature, be forbidden by law, under the severest penalties.

And now I wish here to quote from myself, as there is nothing so true as a prophecy become fact. In the Boston " Advertiser " for November 10, 1871, — mark the day of the month and the year, — appeared an article upon this subject from my pen, in which I said as follows : —

" Let us suppose one of these buildings, say for instance that near the Boston and Maine Railroad, or at Devonshire Street, or that magnificent pile on Tremont and Boylston streets, to be well on fire when the telegraph gave the alarm, in a pleasant and calm day. What a splendid battle there would be between the element of fire and the noble firemen with their beautiful and perfect steam-fire engines ! What a glorious time for the papers ! The dreadful fire with its sheets of flame and its awful clouds of smoke, the intense heat, the falling walls, the wonderful intrepidity of the firemen, the jets of water reaching to the skies, the noise and confusion worse confounded, would make a scene never to be forgotten by those who should be so happy as to see it. It would probably result in a loss only of one building and of

8

a few hundred thousand dollars, for the fire department can do wonders at such a time. Who would not believe that the city was protected from conflagrations, after seeing such a fire kept within the building in which it originated? But let the bells ring the alarm which tells of a fire in one of those buildings when there is such a gale as there was at the Chicago fire, and which there is every month of the year and often every week in Boston. Alas for the doomed city! Place wood, coal, and iron in a blast furnace and set the wood on fire without applying the blast of air. The wood will burn and disappear, while the coal and iron will remain and become cold when the wood has burned out, — but apply the blast of air. The roaring flame of the wood heats the coal to its intense white heat, which melts the iron so that it may be run into moulds of any shape which the ingenuity of man can conceive. It is the air-blast which does this, working upon the elements upon which it is directed. So the furious gale changes in a moment the position of the fire department at a fire. The great building will soon become an awful furnace, the heat of which will prevent the firemen from approaching near it. When the streams rush from the engines they will be beaten to the ground before they can reach the burning building by the power of the wind. The heat soon will become so intense that it will ignite other buildings near it, and in this manner the fire will take the attention of all and more than all of any department. But now comes the real danger.

When that dozen lumber-yards in the roof is once well on fire, it will be taken, not by little sparks only, but by cords, to fall into and upon every building within half a mile! Every window on the line of the gale will be broken into by the fiery brands, every place where there is wood for fire to catch upon, and fires will soon be rushing from fifty of those windows or roaring from the exposed wood. Such a fire (and they will surely occur) will stop just when there is no more wood to burn. The earnest men of the fire department, with their apparatus, would be as inefficient as would the writer with one of his ten-dollar machines. Then would come the story so lately told of Chicago: "Awful conflagration! Boston in ruins! Thousands of houses and the business portion of the city in ashes! Hundreds of men, women, and children burned to death! The people starving! Boston cries for help!" Well, thank God, Boston would have help. The noble-hearted, the truly Christian people of this city have so done their duty to every people in times of distress that the tide of humanity would flow back with interest. But Boston, with its great humanity, its ample means, should, with its splendid schools, teach its people to be more than humane and great-hearted. They should be so intelligent and wise as to be able to guard against such awful calamities as those just described, and which are occurring somewhere almost monthly."

A year afterwards to a day, and Mansard was the best abused Frenchman to be found; but if the people of Boston or any other city content themselves simply with abusing Mansard they have not learned the first lesson of wisdom, which is, — when things go wrong, don't abuse your neighbor, especially if he is dead and buried, but ask yourself what *your* mistake is.

DANGER FROM FIRES IN CHURCHES, HALLS, AND THEATRES.

The danger to public buildings from fire is only too often made known to us through the press. Many theatres and some public halls have been provided with hose, which, coiled up in great unwieldly bundles, would require so long to unroll that before the water could be got on the fire, the fire would have driven the workmen from the building. Extinguishers have also been kept for this use, and are an excellent protection, much better than the great rolls of hose. But the French system is quite the best of any yet known. No performance can take place in any theatre in Paris unless there is on the stage a small fire-engine and two firemen. The scenery may take fire, but there is a dash of water from the engine and all the fire is out in a moment. A small engine, and the workmen in our theatres trained for this purpose, and always at their posts, would insure our theatres from destruction, and might save many hundreds of lives.

BURNING OF THE RICHMOND THEATRE.

This theatre was burned December 16, 1811. Seventy persons perished, including the governor of the State, and many of the first people of Virginia. The fire, when seen by the manager of the theatre, was not two feet in diameter, and with the system I have indicated, would have been extinguished in two or three seconds.

THE DREADFUL CATASTROPHE AT SANTIAGO, CHILI,

By which a church was burned, and two thousand persons perished in the flames, is one of the most awful related in history. The church was illuminated, and decorated with a great number of pictures, etc. A candle fell over and set a picture on fire, which burned slowly for a few moments. The picture was not thirty feet from the floor, and not three feet square. The fire was soon communicated to other pictures and decorations, and then, flying from one to another, it soon set every part of the building on fire. The frightened audience, mostly women, in their fear and haste, closed the doors, which opened inward, and then as the great mass rushed toward the closed doors, they crushed each other to death, or were smothered, or roasted to death by the flames. A little engine and a pail of water would have put out the fire on the painting in a second, and saved two thousand lives.

A very dangerous practice has grown up within a few years of decorating churches, vestries, public halls, etc., with evergreens, at Christmas or for the holidays. The idea is a beautiful one, and if properly managed, that is, if the decorations are taken out in three weeks, it is perfectly safe. But the workers get weary when the fair or the holiday festivals are over, and they are allowed to remain until they are as dry, and much more dangerous, than gunpowder.

Some years since a party of musicians from Europe, after giving concerts in the United States, visited Montreal or Quebec. The audience and the singers were in the hall, when a lamp set one of the dried trees on fire. For half a minute it was quite small, and could have been dashed out

with water if there had been a pump at hand.
Then it flew from one tree to another, and from
one decoration to another, almost with the rapidity
of lightning. The fright and danger became extreme. Many persons were injured, others were
burned, and the building was destroyed.

In 1794 the theatre at Capo d'Istria fell and
crushed the audience and actors in the ruins.

Some years since, when a great musical festival
was given in the Crystal Palace, New York, a
young mechanic, who was there as I was, to sing,
came to me and said, " Do you think the place
upon which we are to sing is strong enough to bear
us ? " " I don't know," said I. " Well," said he,
" I don't believe it is. I am a carpenter, and I
would not allow half the number of people to go
upon it that it is said are expected here to-night."
We went and examined it. Such a flimsy place to
hold thousands of people was never made before,
and I hope never will be again. A man could shake
it back and forth with one hand. We went and
found Mr. Barnum and told him of the danger.
" Well," said he, " what can you do ? " It was
then ten o'clock, and we were to sing that night. I
asked my friend. " Get a thousand of boards, and
a cask of the best nails, and half a dozen men, and
I will see it shored up," said he. They were there
in less than an hour, and the boards were used as

braces in every possible way to strengthen the rickety concern. I don't believe it was possible that we should not have had an awful disaster if it had not been for my Boston friend, nor do I believe it was, though it managed to hold us, half as strong as it should have been, for no building should be erected to sustain great numbers of people which cannot bear up twice the number it can be made to hold. Just preventing a thousand persons from being crushed to death is not enough, when the author of this book is to be one of them.

As buildings grow old, those which were strong enough to bear all the people they could contain when new, will become each season more unsafe. The number of people occupying them increases; and in times of excitement the buildings may become overloaded, and then another sensational disaster will go flying over the telegraph lines.

CHAPTER VIII.

I PROPOSE in this chapter not only to speak of fires which properly come under these heads, but also of those which from their singularity or the peculiar lesson they may teach, it may be well to place in a book of this kind. In 1846, Mr. Braidwood was before a committee of the House of Lords, and said: "It is my belief that by long exposure to heat, not much exceeding that of boiling water at 212°, timber is brought into such a condition that it will take fire without the application of a light. The time during which this process goes on until it ends in spontaneous combustion, is from eight to ten years; so that a fire might be hatching in a man's premises during the whole time of his lease without making any sign!" Now the person whose house is burned up, will say to the insurer, and to the community: "It was not the furnace, the stove, or the steam-pipes, that set the fire; and he will call the carpenter, the mason, and the other mechanics, who will agree with him that it was impossible for fire to take from any such

cause. Then the common people, who like to believe in anything mysterious, believe that there
was something strange about the fire which will
never be explained. The explanation of such fires
I propose to give, and to do it in the most simple
manner, avoiding all words which might mislead
even those who have acquired only the most common education.

It is commonly imagined that the introduction
of hot water, hot air, and steam-pipes as a means
of heating buildings cuts off an avenue of danger
from fire. This is an error. Iron pipes, often
heated up to 400°, are placed in close contact with
floors and skirting boards, supported by slight
diagonal props of wood, which a much lower degree
of heat would suffice to ignite. The circular rim at
Apothecaries Hall which was used in the prepara-
tion of some medicament that required a temperature of only 300°, was found not long ago to have
charred a circle at least a quarter of an inch deep
in the wood beneath it in less than six months.
Mr. Hosking, the author of the " Guide to the
Proper Regulation of Building in Towns," says : —

DAY AND MARTIN'S.

" Day and Martin's blacking manufactory was
heated by means of hot water through iron tubes.
In December, 1848, the wooden casing, etc., was

found to be on fire. The only cause to be discovered was the exposure for a long time of the wood to the heated pipes."

The pipes were not in contact with the wooden casing, but they were stayed and kept upright by cross fillets of wood which touched them, and these it was which appeared to have taken fire. In every case where the prop which held the pipe from the floor had been displaced, *the boards were charred.*

DANGER FROM DRIED WOOD.

" Wood dried in the thorough manner we have mentioned is so liable to catch fire from flame that practical men imagine there must be some kind of atmosphere surrounding it of a highly imflammable nature. A stick of pine-wood thrust into a fire will emit from its free end a volatile spirit of turpentine, which lights like a jet of gas." That this *vapor* has been the cause of many fires I have no doubt. Fires in drying-houses often occur, and the reason has not been found. How easy it would be for a little cloud of such vapor to float off to a light, or to the furnace, to be lighted, and to return to the dried wood a living flame, which would, in five minutes, set the whole building in a blaze. Many other buildings than dry-houses have, I think, been fired in that manner.

DANGER FROM VAPOR.

That a vapor rises from inflammable oils is well understood; but there are, as we have seen in wood, doubtless others, arising from many things heated for drying or. for some other purposes. In 1866 we are told of a fire in a wool-drying room: " He entered the room with his lantern. Soon after leaving he smelt smoke, and opening the wool-drying room, he found it full of smoke. As soon as the air was admitted the fire flashed all over the room at once, as by flashes of lightning." In 1868 a similar fire occurred in a room for drying wool: " The watchman entered it with his lantern. Leaving it for a moment, he wished to return, but found it full of fire, and was obliged to escape by a window."

SPONTANEOUS COMBUSTION IS AT PRESENT VERY LITTLE UNDERSTOOD.

The London " Quarterly " for January, 1855, says: " The cause of most fires from this source is lost in the consequence." That is, the engines arrive so late that the signs of the cause are burned up. " A porter swept the sawdust from the floor into a heap, upon which the oil (olive) from a broken flask dripped. The sun shone on the heap, and in sixteen hours it took fire."

OILED RAGS, COTTON AND COTTON-WASTE, HEMP, ETC.

Extracts from Mr. Braidwood: " Spontaneous ignition is believed to be a very fruitful cause of fires, but unless the fire is discovered almost at its commencement it is difficult to ascertain that this is the cause. It is generally accelerated by natural or artificial heat. Sawdust, cotton, cotton-waste, hemp, and most other vegetable substances wet with oil are very likely to take fire. The serious fires in the railroad stations about London have most of them commenced in the paint stores. In a large fire in an oil warehouse a quantity of oil was spilled the day before and wiped up, and the wipings thrown aside. They were believed to have been the cause of the fire. No collection of rubbish or lumber of any sort should be allowed to be made in any building of value."

A fire in Fall River was a mystery until Mr. Eddy, who had the care of the building, found that in a board just over the pipes were several pitch knots. The turpentine distilled from the knots and fell upon the pipe, and took fire from its heat and set the building on fire. An iron pipe containing steam not under pressure, packed in shavings, passed overhead in a saw-mill. The shavings took fire and the mill was destroyed.

Dr. C. T. Jackson supposed the turpentine distilled from the shavings. A box containing fine sawdust was placed around a pipe conveying steam from one mill to another. The box was on fire a great number of times. There were twelve fires in the city of Philadelphia in a year, ending March, 1868, in woolen mills, from these and similar causes. Two fires from oily waste occurred in Hartford.

Some clean woolen waste was once taken from a mill and stored in a warehouse in Pearl Street. The insurance companies notified the agent to remove it. Objection to this was made, when Mr. Gould placed some of it in a yard in State Street. This was in August. It took fire in less than twenty-four hours. Many other cases of woolen mills could be stated, but these are sufficient to warn persons of the danger.

The house of Mrs. Colburn, at Cambridge, took fire from woolen rags saturated with linseed oil. Another fire at Cambridge was from the following cause : At a house where were a number of workmen one was using oiled rags. When the dinner-bell rang he put his rags into his overalls, and taking them off he threw them into a closet. Before one o'clock a workman, who providentially ate his dinner in the house, smelt fire. He found the oiled rags had set the overalls on fire, and soon the house would have been on fire also.

A fine house in Cambridge was destroyed a few years ago. Cause first, oiled rags ; second, no small engine, — it was discovered when one could have put out the fire ; third, when the people were called where the telegraph box was kept the key could not be found. I could give several other reasons, but an old anecdote will perhaps be more pleasant reading. One of the crowned heads of Europe, while passing through one of his cities, was not saluted, as is the custom. Some time afterward the mayor of the city appeared at court to apologize for the want of respect shown to his majesty. "Sire," said the mayor, "I have one hundred reasons why we could not fire a salute." "Well," said the king, "what is the first reason." "We had no powder, sire." "That will answer," said the good-natured monarch, and he left the mayor to get out of the palace as he best could.

It is a singular fact that while I was looking up these and many other cases in Cambridge, a person was as busy trying to prove that fires could not be set by oiled rags, and he made many converts. I found one instance in a furniture warehouse, where a handful of oiled rags thrown on a bench, on a hot day in August, took fire in fifteen minutes !

A singular case of fire was discovered at the library of the Philosophical Society, George Street, Manchester, England. On entering the room one afternoon a sofa was seen to be on fire. It was taken into the yard and the fire extinguished, when the sofa was found to have been stuffed with waste woolen material from the mills, which, being oily, had taken fire.

A vessel loaded with wool was set on fire by a flask of oil broken in the cabin. The oil dripped through the floor upon the wool, and the fire commenced.

A great building in State Street was destroyed by fire a few years since from the following cause : In the basement near the front of the store there was a large tank, in which was kept varnish. While filling it from casks the vapor, which sometimes is in such tanks, was forced out into the cellar. Floating along, as does the smoke we sometimes see in the air before a storm, it slowly worked its way to the other end of the cellar, where there was a lighted jet of gas. The moment it touched the gas it ran back, a river of fire, which drove the men out of the cellar, set the varnish on fire, and in an incredibly short time had set the whole building on fire, and in spite of the spirited exertions of the firemen it was totally destroyed. A building was erected on the same lot, and soon another fire occurred in it, which should also show the need of caution and care of all persons engaged in such stores. A lot of linseed oil in barrels was stored in the third loft from the street. One of them leaked, and the oil ran along the floor thirty or forty feet, until it leaked through and fell into a barrel of lamp-black in papers. This at once, of course, took fire, but it was discovered in time to save most of the building.

It is a rule in most of the furniture warehouses, where oiled rags are used, to burn them every night in winter, but in the summer, when there is no fire, they are thrown into the water. Then they are picked up by boys, and sold into the junk shops. Probably not a few of the many fires so common in such stores arise from these rags from the furniture stores.

A very nice lamp-black may be gathered from the gas jet under the glue-pots of such establishments. But great care is necessary, as it takes fire very easily. One of the men was told to be careful of it by a foreman one day, and sure enough it was then on fire in his hands.

The following is an extract from " Fires and Fire Systems ": " Spontaneous combustion is the power of ignition inherent in animal and vegetable substances. The putrefaction of vegetables is known to occasion the development of so much heat as sometimes to cause their ignition. It has been proved that hemp, jute, cotton, flax, etc., when they are stored in a damp cellar, or left in a state

9

of grease or oily dirt, may take fire." Mr. Old-
ham, of the Bank of England, knew of three fires
caused by greasy rags lying together. It was his
opinion that they would sometimes take fire after
they had lain safely for a year. I once knew of a
fire said to have been set by an incendiary, but
which I have no doubt caught from oiled rags,
some of which had lain where the fire caught for
many months. In 1858 a·quantity of asphalted
felt, stored in a yard at Camberwell, ignited, but
was seen and at once extinguished. In a few
weeks it was on fire again. " A heap of fine charcoal ten feet square and four feet deep, in three
days was heated to 90° from 57°. On the sixth
day it had risen to 150°, and on the seventh day
it had taken fire in several places."

Dr. Jackson says : " Three times I have set fire
to charcoal at temperatures less than boiling water.
My first experiment was accidental. I took a
flask filled with gunpowder and laid it on a stove
to dry. I then took a paper of pulverized charcoal, such as is sold by apothecaries for tooth powder, the charcoal being wrapped in white paper,
and placed it on the top of the gunpowder which
was being dried upon the stove. Having occasion
to go out, I took off the paper of charcoal and laid
it upon the table. When I came back, in about
twenty minutes, I observed the paper smoking.

The charcoal was completely consumed. During all this time the gunpowder remained on the stove unexploded."

The next experiment is thus told : " I had occasion to use a piece of charcoal for blow-pipe experiments. I went down into my cellar and brought up a piece of light, fine, round charcoal, suited for that purpose. It was damp. I laid it on the top of a column stove to dry, directly by a tin pan containing water, which was not boiling, and never did boil there. I took the charcoal off the stove and laid it on my table. A short time afterwards I discovered it was on fire all through the piece. I laid it aside and it burned entirely to ashes." " I repeated this experiment again, watching it carefully, and with the same result." Now let us see what the practical working of this would be. The wood under a stove has, by continued heating, become charcoal. It is covered with an oil-cloth carpet and an iron or zinc plate. The charcoal takes fire, and as it cannot burn up through the carpet and iron plate, it burns down to the space below the floor. From thence it goes off in any direction of the draft to the side of the building, and then upwards, perhaps, even to the roof, where the fire is first seen, or in any of the stories, as the case may be. Such a fire, in the daytime, may result in a damage of from a hundred to thousands of dollars. In the night the building is often a total loss. The papers will report the fires, " it was seen near the stove," or it was first seen in the third, fourth, or fifth story, or the attic, as the case may be, or " the building seemed to be on fire from the basement to the attic." These fires are preparing all over the city. No careful man will ever put up a stove in such a way, but he allows his workmen to do it for him.

A few years ago I went with my wife to one of the great wholesale clothing houses in Boston. I had occasion to go out of an errand, and when I returned she said to me, " I think there has been some kind of fire in that opposite room." " Why ? " " Well, there was quite a smoke and a running of men, and water was carried in there." Of course that was the place for me, and in I went. A kind of tailor's furnace had been put up that morning, fire-proof of course, and in the first three hours it had set the building on fire. Just suppose that it could have waited a few hours, until any time from twelve o'clock at night to three or four in the morning. The story would have been, " A great fire in —— Street; loss $500,000." I suppose I meddled with somebody's business, and made some person angry with me, for I at once told the firm of it. No such machine was ever put up after that, without being carefully examined by them. In this way we fail to "rely enough upon ourselves, but trust too much to others."

All over our stores, workshops, warehouses, and in many dwelling-houses, the stove, furnace, steam or hot water-pipes or gas-jets, are turning the wood to charcoal. The causes of spontaneous ignition in London, in 1859, were, charcoal, felt tarred, and phosphorus, one each; wet hemp, ropes, and mats, sulphur and saltpetre, two each; cotton waste, three; greasy rubbish, four; lampblack and oily rags, seven each.

The English books on this subject do not mention woolen rags with oil, nor do the Boston Fire Department reports often speak of them. Yet they are certainly one of the most prominent causes of danger. The following from "Fires in Woolen Mills," from which are many of the extracts in this chapter, should be remembered by every person: "Managers and workmen should know that spontaneous combustion is not an accidental phenomenon. With the proper conditions it is as certain as the firing of gunpowder with a spark. The cask of gunpowder will not explode till the spark is applied. The pile of oily waste, harmless and innocent to all appearance, slowly but surely takes from the oxygen of the air the means for its own combustion, itself lighting the

conflagration, which most frequently bursts forth
when manager and operatives are locked in slum-
ber ; " or father, mother, and children, if in a
dwelling.

NEW CAUSES OF SPONTANEOUS IGNITION.

We now know of many causes, but it cannot be
doubted that others will yet be discovered which
have set fires and are not yet suspected. A few
years since a freshet filled the basement of a large
machine shop in the western part of the State.
There were in the room many turning-lathes for
turning iron and steel. At the bottom of many
of them were piles of steel and iron waste. This
is the refuse cut or filed from the work while fin-
ishing it, and it is well saturated with oil. There
had always been such heaps there, but when the
water was drawn off, the heaps of iron dross and.
oil, left wet with water, began to steam, and
soon they were wheeled out for safety on to a
waste place, where the heap became red hot inside ! A new combination for fire setting ! A
young woman in a house in my neighborhood
thought there was a smell of fire in one of the
rooms. Looking about she saw smoke rising from·
the centre-table, and upon it she found a line
which had been burned, the end of which was
then on fire. Calling in the family, it was seen

that the globe on the table, in which were swimming about a pair of gold fish, was in the rays of the sun, and had become a burning glass, and was busily at work as an incendiary! Round glass paper-weights have also, by the aid of the sun, become fire-setters. No such shaped glass should be placed where the rays of the sun may strike it.

Some of the many fires in the forests are supposed to be set by the sun shining upon the gum, which oozing from the trees sometimes is formed into the proper shape, thus becoming a sun-burner. Very likely, but nine out of ten of them are from the laziness of persons who go into the woods, make fires, and go off without extinguishing them.

And this leads to an important item for a book of this kind. How many fires are a consequence of burning of the waste of a garden, etc., near the buildings. Wheel them away, and set them on fire where they will be quite out of danger. And never set any waste on fire on a windy day. Well do I recollect seeing the smoke of a fire at Dedham. The servant was told to set fire to some waste in the afternoon. The wind had arisen then, and it was unsafe. But obey orders was the word, and soon the waste and a fine mansion were on fire, which came near burning other valuable buildings. Always have an engine with

water when you make such fires about the place.
If wanted for nothing else they will put out the
fire and so prevent danger. If water is scarce,
cover up the remains of the fire with dirt. I have
known several fires for neglecting these cautions.
There was one in Cambridge a year ago. Sometimes the grass takes fire about a house or barn in
a dry time. If there is a high wind, and the fire
is near the building, a pail of water and a dipper
will almost always wet about the building enough
to keep it from catching. A small engine, however, will in this case do wonders. Some one once
told me that the grass was on fire near my barn,
when in a minute I was there with a pail and little
engine. No one could have been more surprised
than myself at the instant beating out of the flame
for about forty feet each way. But in the country,
when the grass is on fire for many rods and running in every direction, stick right to your own
buildings until the fire is out there, and then help
your neighbors. Women should always avoid
going near where those fires are burning, as the
blaze often starts up after it has been dashed out
by brush or even water, and there would be danger
of their clothes taking fire. People too often do
great injustice to those who make fires in stores.
A store is on fire near the stove. The boy who
has charge of the fire is suspected of doing it by

carelessness. I was telling a merchant of these things, when he with the most earnest manner said that he had now no doubt that he had once wronged a poor boy in that way.

A fire of any kind occurs, and it seems as if the very devil himself set even good Christians to give any origin for it but the true one. By giving a true statement of all fires, we should soon know almost exactly their cause, and thus be able to prevent them. This would be even better than using small engines !

INCENDIARY FIRES.

There are many kinds of incendiary fires.

Malicious incendiarism, or setting fire to revenge some supposed personal injury, has in all ages been known as a crime. It, however, very rarely occurs; and the fact that a person is so wickedly disposed toward the man whose buildings are destroyed, often leads to his conviction and punishment.

FRAUDULENT INCENDIARISM.

This kind of incendiarism is in some countries and cities very common. It prevails in the cities of England, and in this and other countries. In New York some of the insurance companies have been compelled to refuse to insure certain classes of people. The Irish people, to their credit be it

written, stand well in this respect. The fire mar-
shals' reports of that city give startling figures of
such fires.

PYROMANIA.

This kind of incendiarism, called in England
Monomania, though very rare, when it does occur
causes great fright and trouble to the families and
friends of the person so afflicted. In London, a
boy of fifteen set fire to his father's premises seven
times in one day. A girl, while on a visit to her
friends, set fire to the bed-curtains, to the window-
blinds, to the curtains of the windows of five rooms,
the kitchen towels, a bed, and when the bedclothes
were removed to the coach-house for safety, they
were set on fire there five times. Furniture, books,
and indeed everything almost which would burn,
were set fire to. Fortunately the fires were seen
when small, and easily extinguished; and at last
the incendiary was caught in the act of setting
fire. There was no possible motive, and pyromania was the only excuse.

This crime, or disease, is much more prevalent
in this country than in others. In Europe, it was
almost always persons from fifteen to twenty years
of age. In this country, children of from eight to
fifteen have been afflicted with it; and it is quite
certain that persons have set fire after fire in towns
where there were no engines, and where there

could be no possible reason except this pyromania. Houses, barns, school-houses, and churches have been burned, in out of the way villages, miles away from engines, and where no motive of revenge or any other could be conceived. Little boys, and even girls, have set fire to the property of their parents, and of others; and while the neighbors supposed them to be awful children, physicians, and those who knew the facts of this disease, saw that they were suffering a dreadful infliction.

INCENDIARISM FOR DEVILTRY.

This dreadful crime, which was unknown in this country until the introduction of " suction engines," as they were called, about 1830, was quite common in ancient Rome. " The rivalries of the various companies of ancient firemen continually caused disturbances and rows, just as was the case in London prior to 1830, and in some of the cities of America at the present day." The punishment of death was awarded to all who willfully fired buildings, from the very earliest period. In ancient Rome, where the crime was very common, those found guilty were burned to death, by placing them in a sack covered with pitch, etc., which, once on fire, gave the criminal no chance of escape. In this country, the excitement attending the rivalries of engine companies, causing incendiarism, was increased, until the rate of insurance was more than twice what it would have been but for that cause. Fires were set everywhere and at all times; but not a Saturday night could pass in the neighborhood of several crack companies, as they were termed, without one, two, or three fires. In a town near Boston, where there was an old, small engine, years ago, the young men formed a company, and the town gave them a splendid new one. In the next fifteen years the town was dotted all over with the ruins of buildings set on fire by " the boys," to call engines from other towns, so that they might have the pleasure of " sucking them or running them over ! " At the same time the young men — that is, those who " run wid der machine," — grew more and more immoral, until it was at last impossible for them to find a lower position. One night, when one of the out-of-town engines had been badly beaten, one of the members, who had learned that an improved means for throwing water had been invented, proposed that their engine should be supplied with it. It was done, and within two days there was a fire in that village, and the new made-up engine " walloped " the old victorious one most unmercifully. This last was taken home, put in perfect order, and immediately a fire in that town was the result;

but when the engines got to work, the old splendid engine was beaten by the one with the new works as badly as before.

For all this fun and these exciting trials, somebody's premises were burned by incendiary fires. But now a challenge was given to try the two machines. The result was that the "new works" triumphed at every trial. The other engine was taken home, the company disbanded, and there was but one fire in the town for a year, and that one accidental, and the loss not $100! But at last there was an anxiety about the safety of the town! A company must be raised. The old people said, "Keep quiet, and you will have no fires;" but the boys at last formed a company and took the engine, which was painted up and put in fine order. Some unwise persons said there would be a fire the next Saturday night. There was none, nor for the next two Saturday nights, and the engine boys said: "Now what do you think of the stories you have been telling about us?" But alas! the incendiary had been all this time growing, and the next Saturday, and for five successive ones, there were incendiary fires in that town! I do not suppose one of the fires was set by a member of the company; but it matters little to the family whose house and barn or workshop is destroyed, who has set it; it is the

loss which they feel. The steam fire-engine
that town at once killed off and choked
growth of the crime, let us hope, forever. '
engine excitement became a national calam
It took our good boys from the schools, wl
they were taught good morals as well as read
etc., and placed them in engine-houses, where t
were taught to be rowdies, roughs, and wh
unfit members of engine companies or of soci
When they were disbanded from the engine,
a new company formed, it also grew in a few y
as bad as the first, and so new companies were
moralized every five or six years.   The cri
committed at Baltimore, Philadelphia, and]
York by engine-companies would, if told, astoɪ
and fill with dismay those who should read th
Even here, in and about good old puritanical]
England, it was dreadful. I have seen a
house but little on fire — which could have been
out in two or three minutes with the smallest ha
engine, and yet when there was a line ·formeɩ
large engines all ready to play upon it — burː
the ground, because in the middle of that
there was an engine a little less powerful than
rest, and she was taken out and another puɪ
her place, that there might be a fair trial of
engines. Hundreds of fires, aye thousands of bu
ings have been destroyed in that wicked manne

At a fire near Boston, on a Saturday night in 1854, where the loss was $150,000, the engines had got the fire almost out where it begun, but the engine drafting from the nearest reservoir was sucked by a more powerful one. The cry was raised, "the reservoir has given out," and the line broken up. Before another line was formed, half a dozen buildings were on fire, and the loss was as above stated. But as more distant engines arrived, one of them dropped her suction hose into that reservoir, and found water enough there to supply a line all the time of the fire! At the same fire, when it had lit upon a large building, and was quite small, a line was formed, and broken, that it might be *a fair fight*, and the fire, who never plays make believe, was all over the house before the new line was ready to play, when the battle began, and was a splendid one. I do not know which engine conquered, but I do know that the valuable house was destroyed, though it could have been saved with a hand-pump with ease. There were at one time in the prison at Charlestown, twenty-three convicts, sent there for this crime of incendiarism. At the commencement of the last war, a large number of young men in this State were told that if they would enlist in the army, the grand jury would be saved some trouble, and their friends from disgrace.

They enlisted! It would seem perhaps a pity to tell these stories, and I would not, if there was not reason for it. The old fire departments after the introduction of the suction hose, were got up in all honesty of purpose to extinguish fires. To save yours, mine, every person's property, and yet the tendency of it was such that more property was destroyed than ever. More fires were set by our own children, our boys, — who but for the fire system, would have been good young men, — than the Indians ever set for us in all the Indian wars; yes, a hundred to one! Nor, if there was blame at all, were the young men as much to blame as the miserable town officers, who, knowing of these evils, upheld the system, that they might hold their petty office. This same system is still upheld in many towns. Incendiaries are still grown with as much certainty as is a crop of potatoes, or corn. The lurid sky by night, the great smoke by day, tell in hundreds of places in our country of the awful curse of the old-fashioned custom of playing into each other by fire-engines. The lines would seldom be formed until too late to save a building, and the excitement and rivalry were the greatest cause of the fires.

The steam-engines have been a blessing wherever they have been introduced, when drawn by horses, for they have put out fires, and squelched this kind of incendiarism. But let us see the result when drawn by men. A town near Boston purchased a steam fire-engine. They also kept in commission one or two manual engines. The steamer required fifty or sixty men, and the others only twenty or thirty to draw them to the fire. Of course the small manual would be at the fire and at work, taking the honors from the steamer every time, — and for this fires were set every week! Horses were furnished for the steamer, and she was put to work first, when the fires ceased. The remedy for this, the worst kind of incendiarism, is to do away with the old manual system of suction engines. The best remedy for other kinds, is the introduction of small engines. At present the proof of a fire being set, is burned up before the great engines can be got to work; but if water could be got on the fire in one or two minutes after it was discovered, the means employed by the incendiary would almost always be saved, and be witnesses against him. No man would set his house on fire to save his insurance, if the chances were ten to one that the fire would be put out in two or three minutes, and that instead of his insurance he would get ten or a dozen years in the state prison.

10

CHAPTER IX.

SYSTEMS, NEW AND OLD.

FIRE INSURANCE.

IT is within the memory of many people, when insurance against fire was unknown except in a few large cities. If a fire occurred, their townsmen gave the sufferers what would relieve their present need, though seldom enough to keep them from future want and suffering. Therefore when it became known that for a few dollars per annum, the buildings of a farm, or of the merchant or mechanic, would be replaced, if destroyed by fire, there was an almost universal resort to that excellent means of safety. This result was hastened, when some person, who was not insured, suffered a loss, and when his neighbors were called upon, as in past times, for aid, gave for answer, "He might have had his buildings insured." In those times buildings were seldom so crowded together, built so high, or in any way so out of the reach of the fire departments. Nor were there then the friction match, the inflammable oils, or the dozen other fire-setting materials which in our times have been introduced, or worst of all, the incendiarism for fun, bread and cheese and rum, which for years was the great curse of our country, and which is to this day one of the most prolific causes of fire in the country.

The business of the insurance offices was managed with economy, and the result was that the insured were sure of their money if their buildings were destroyed, while insurance stock was one of the safest investments for those who had money, and immense amounts of the property of widows and orphans were placed in them as the safest and most profitable investment which could be made for them. For many years this pleasant state of things continued, but it is hardly possible for such perfection to last forever in this sphere, and the invention of matches and the increase of the use of pipes a thousand fold, with oils and chemicals, the dangerous nature of which was unknown to many who had to use them, increased both the number and magnitude of fires. Of course the rate of insurance also increased, and the fires and rates at last became a burden. All this while, buildings with tarred paper and tinder-wood roofs were climbing heavenward out of the reach of fire departments, and so when at last the destruction of cities became an annual sensation, and the insurance companies went up with them, the people who lost by them laid all the burden upon the insurance companies as if they already had not enough of their own to bear. The insurance people made a grave mistake when they insured those fire-traps at all. Twenty per cent. per annum, will not be a safe premium for a city or town, where those buildings are near together, and where the only protection is steam fire-engines. But why throw all the shot at the poor insurance companies. We have not heard a word against the merchants whose property was destroyed by fire in the cities of Chicago and Boston. Yet they were as much at fault as the others. The merchants were unfortunate, and so were the companies, with this difference, that the companies warned the merchants not to build such dangerous warehouses. We ridicule the fashions of the women, but they all for the past century have not cost as much as the great fires from dangerous roofs have in a few years; nor have they ever had a fashion even on their heads so ridiculous as the great high buildings of six or more stories with the roof composed of tarred paper and pine-boards. Insurance people are not perfect, as there is no perfection here. There are in their number— well what there are in every class of men. But nowhere, in any business class of people, will you find more intelligent, courteous, liberal, fair-minded men, more willing to do entire justice, nay, to help those who have suffered by fire, than the officers of insurance companies. They are careful, and if not we must all lose by them. They sometimes seem to suspect persons, or ask questions which may seem to do so. But this they have learned to do from their intercourse with customers who too often are not honest men.

I cannot answer for the companies at Chicago; but I know that the officers of the Boston companies, as gentlemen and careful, conscientious business men, rank, in mercantile phrase, A No. 1, when compared with any other class in the community.

I read lately in a journal that the rate of insurance had been raised in Boston and in New York. I not only see the necessity of it, but I also believe that unless we can have our present buildings made more safe, more indestructible, and our fire departments sooner at work at fires, with the rates doubled, it will not continue to be a safe business, or a proper investment for the property of widows and orphans. It may be so for a few years, perhaps, but it also is liable to almost instant destruction from conflagrations which no department is able to control in a high wind. "Unstable as the wind;" yet the entire property of millions of the people of the United States is at the mercy of the elements.

Will the present season of great fires continue in the future? This question is often asked by persons who hope that the present apparent high tide of fires will soon cease, and that we may soon have no more than there were ten, twenty, or forty years ago. But there is no reason for such hope. On the contrary, unless there is some decided change in the manner of erecting buildings, or of arresting fires, the fire records will grow longer, and the figures of losses increase in number.

We are a new country. Timber has been so cheap that we have built wholly almost of it; or if we have built what we call brick, stone, or iron structures, there is so much wood about them that once on fire they are as easily destroyed as if only of wood.

Our towns and the outer portions of our cities have been usually laid out into large house-lots, with the dwelling-house in the centre and surrounded by beautiful trees and flowers, while somewhere in the rear, the good man could find room for most of the vegetables for the use of the family.

Fires when they happened in such situations burned a house without much danger to others. One building lost at a fire created no great alarm to the inhabitants, nor raised the rate of insurance. But a gradual change is taking place all over the

country. The delightful gardens are sold off for
house-lots, a person often selling a lot for a house
on each side of his own ; here and there a great
manufactory looms up, and in a few years streets
with beautiful residences environed by trees and
flowers have become thickly settled, with buildings
on the streets and with shops and stables, etc., in
their rear, thus more than quadrupling the danger
of fires. So long as this filling up process continues, the number of our fires will also increase ;
and when they are sufficiently crowded together,
and a fire occurs at the same time that there is a
gale of wind, we shall have conflagrations. Perhaps it is only by dreadful conflagrations that a
people can be taught to construct buildings which
cannot be burned. If this is true we are having
at present the teaching process laid pretty heavily
upon us. It will be sure, however, to increase.
Conflagration after conflagration will be as sure
to follow each other as any other effect follows its
cause. Would it not be a cheaper, a less disastrous
way of bringing about reforms in this direction, to
look carefully about us, and see if we may not
build so safely as to hardly require fire departments, or if we have any, that we may have them
at the fire on the instant of its discovery. Until
we do make these changes we may be assured that
the fires will rapidly increase, and that the rate of

insurance will be forced upward as fast as the fires grow in number and magnitude.

We see such evils in our common business avocations. When a machine does not work, or a stove or furnace does not heat, we alter or change them. If our pen, our paper, our ink is poor we discard them for some other. If our iron, steel, or if anything fails to satisfy us, we away with it and get what will answer our purpose. Are we satisfied; do we feel safe with our high Mansard roofs, our crowded wooden buildings; or are we like the Wapping fishwomen, and like a good fire once in a while just for a change. If that is true we are a very happy people. If we are not pleased with the fires, let us look to ourselves for the remedy.

The dreadful fires of San Francisco and other cities of the gold regions afford a lesson from which all persons living in cities and large towns may obtain a knowledge, which should enable them to shun the danger of fires, by erecting buildings which will not easily take fire and be destroyed. The first great fire was in December, 1849, and the loss was $1,500,000. The next was May 4, 1850. Loss was $3,000,000. There was another July 14, the loss of which was $5,000,000; and there were four other large fires the same year.

May 3, 1851, two thousand five hundred buildings were burned in less than nine hours, and the loss was $17,000,000. Another fire on the 22d June, destroyed property valued at $3,000,000.

November 12, 1852, the city of Sacramento was burned. Ten lives were lost, and two thousand buildings were burned. The loss was $12,000,000.

The city of Nevada was burned, with the loss of $1,200,000.

May 14, 1851, the town of Stockton was destroyed. Loss $10,000,000. There were also other large fires in these, and other towns in the golden regions, amounting in all to several millions of dollars. Such is a brief history of the disastrous fires in those new cities, which sent a thrill of horror through the United States.

As at Chicago, money, provisions, building material, in short, everything which could be of use to the sufferers, was sent with an unsparing hand. And now for the lesson.

When the people arrived in California, they commenced to erect a city. But there was no proper material with which to build one which would be safe from destruction from fire. They therefore put up thousands of buildings of light boards, and of lath and plaster; and the partitions were of calico, shirting, sheeting, and even paper. These were crowded together, in a country subject to high winds and droughts, and of course, where there was no fire department. Of course, also, the cities were destroyed in less hours or minutes than they were days in building. They were rebuilt in the same manner and with the same result. Then when the ground was once more covered with the same material, or nearly so, the eastern cities had sent fire apparatus, and a "splendid fire department" was the consequence. Then came another fire, and before the department could get to work, whole streets of light wood, cotton cloth and paper were on fire, and the department was forced to seek safety by keeping out of the way of the devouring element.

At length the people discovered that if they were to have a city, it must be built of brick and stone; and when they had at last succeeded in erecting such buildings, and perfecting their fire department, the conflagrations ceased to destroy them. Still another lesson should be learned from these western fires. After the first fires the buildings were not all of boards, cotton cloth, and paper. Many fine warehouses were erected, only to be destroyed in the great conflagrations caused by the cheap structures others had put up, as at first. People must not only erect substantial buildings, but the law must require that only such shall be made if a city is to be safe from destruction from fire.

It was the careless manner of building which was the cause of the conflagrations of Chicago and Boston. Will those cities now rebuild so that fire can never obtain the mastery over them? I fear not.

A very few dangerous buildings, with open elevators, and filled with great quantities of inflammable goods, may cause the destruction of a city in a furious gale of wind.

There must be strict laws against dangerous buildings, and regulations for dangerous merchandise. There must be an ever watchful care over the fire departments, or they may, though composed of excellent men and with good material, be formed upon a system which will render them wholly inefficient.

There is no danger that the ridiculous manner of building which destroyed the golden cities will ever be attempted in this section of the country; but the conflagrations of Chicago and Boston, and the hundreds of fires in every direction, indicate that we must build more safely and improve our fire-preventive systems, or conflagrations will continue to afflict us and in such a degree as to affect our prosperity as a nation.

The great conflagration in New York of December 16, 1835 — when six hundred buildings, great warehouses and stores were burned, involving a loss of near $20,000,000 — was caused by the narrow streets, a gale of wind, and the intense cold which froze up the engines, and rendered them useless.

The next great fire occurred July 19, 1845. The loss was thirty-five men killed, and $5,000,000. The cause was a terrible explosion of saltpetre, which destroyed the building and two or three others. Near two hundred warehouses were burned. It commenced in a box factory, which was next the warehouse containing the saltpetre.

How many such dangerous places are there at the present time in our cities and large towns. Tinder-boxes adjoining warehouses filled with saltpetre, inflammable oils, or some other dangerous substances, endangering whole cities.

THE ALBANY FIRE.

In Albany, August 1846, a fire commenced in a small stable. The day was intensely hot. The wind blew a hurricane, and the fire soon raged with dreadful fury. It at length came toward several stables full of hay with great numbers of combustible buildings about them. A little water would have checked it there, but alas, the engines were all engaged elsewhere; it was a one-idea department: little engines which could have arrested the fire were not used, and "onward sped the fire!" Then again, the sparks flew away on the wings of the wind two hundred rods from the conflagration, and soon another conflagration was at its fiery work. Tow and canal boats, schooners on the river, and five hundred houses with vast quantities of merchandise, were destroyed. From what city will the next great fire disaster send its dreadful story to the world? When will the papers tell, "that though there was a gale, a drought, and the fire flew over and set fires on the line of the wind for miles, the small engines dashed them out in a minute or two, and the splendid steamers, when the fire came to an open space or square, succeeded in arresting its progress with the loss of but a few thousands of dollars." Echo answers — When?

It would be easy to continue these notices of fires until they filled volumes. But any person who would not be convinced with these, would never be so. Suffice it to say, that if it is high winds which makes great fires, we must find something which can compete with fires in a high wind, if it is crowded wooden buildings, we must not crowd them; if it is oils, saltpetre, etc., we must place them where they will be safe, or at least will not expose the property of others if on fire.

HOW MAY GREAT CONFLAGRATIONS BE EXTINGUISHED?

Not a little has been written and said of the inefficiency of the Boston firemen, when the fire, once having the mastery, was racing, roaring away in four different directions; and when from twenty to thirty, forty, fifty, seventy, or a hundred buildings were on fire at once, and most of them setting fire to others. One large building on fire adjoining others requires six or ten engines to make everything safe all about it; and at the same rate, there were needed hundreds at the Boston fire. I do not think it was possible to procure steamers enough, nor do I think there was water enough for them, if they could have been there in season. Great conflagrations, especially in a gale, usually burn through a town or a city, to the open land, or to water, if there is any. There were many places where the steamers made a stand against the fire, and where the firemen worked like heroes, only to be driven away, and see millions destroyed which they hoped and nobly labored to save. There were many other places where, when all the steamers were employed in other situations, the fire slowly approached, and at last the heat, or sparks, set a little fire, and as there was nothing at all to extinguish it with, another fire was kindled, and went off on its fiery work of destruction. For this the department was not at all at fault. They worked with such engines and water as the city furnished them with. Few can understand the great difficulties under which the chief engi-

neer and his assistants labored. Hundreds of merchants whose property was doomed to destruction,
crowding about them frantic for aid and engines;
then engines coming in all directions, asking where
to be placed; the fire every moment changing its
front, or breaking out in new places, — created a
confusion, and often a panic, which would excuse
any one for doubting what to do, or for an error of
judgment, when he did give an order. More
than this, at such times a very proper order may
be given, and before it can be executed, the fire
may so change that it would be the height of folly
to attempt to perform the duty. For myself, I
don't know what I could have done; and I am sure
I have not a word to say against the engineer and
his assistants at the fire, but think there was a
great deal to commend. I think, however, that it
will soon be found that the best time to attempt
to work at conflagrations will be when they are
about three feet in diameter!

In this statement I think all those who suffered
at the great fire, and their friends, will agree with
me.

The people of Boston have been generous toward their firemen, and the expense of the department, however great, has never been grudged;
but more than this is necessary for their safety
from fire. They must not only be willing to pay,

but they must also look into the subject of fires,
and insist that if fires cannot now be attacked in
season to prevent conflagrations, by the present
method, we must introduce others which can instantly attack them when small, and extinguish
them at once.

A great number of firemen, with a great many
steam-fire engines poured an immensity of water
on hundreds of buildings on fire or in danger of
taking fire; and at last, with almost infinite labor
the fire in the hundreds of buildings was drowned
out — after ten million times as much labor as
would have been required — by one or two little
engines in the roof of the second building burned!

There has been no great fire like that of Boston.
Conflagrations usually commence with wooden
buildings as at Chicago, and the sparks flying
on the wind drop on other buildings, setting fire
to them faster than the great engines can be
moved to them.   Not so this great fire of Boston.
The portion of the city where the fire began was
almost entirely covered with Mansard roofs. Away
up, out of the reach of the engines, they most of
them were made of wood, boards on the frame,
tarred paper on that, over which were slates.
Added to that was the fact that the streets led
every which way, to use a country expression. In
a gale of wind, when the engines could not reach

to the roof, there was nothing to save the city.
But there was no high wind. It was a quiet night.
Of course when fifty or a hundred great buildings
filled with immense quantities of inflammable goods.
were on fire, a draft was created, which came to the
fire from every direction. A gentleman testified
that his hat was violently blown toward the fire.
Looking up, he saw the whole course of the smoke
and sparks passing over him in the opposite direction. His hat would have blown north, south, or
east, if he had been on those sides of the fire. In
Paris, and other places in Europe where there are
Mansard roofs on high buildings, they are not
made to burn, but are of substances indestructible
by fire. It may be said that the steamers should
have thrown water upon the roofs. But they
did not, and the question is, What other protection
can we have ?

The heat of a large building may be so intense
that no man can live in the street near enough to
it to throw water upon a roof opposite the fire.
A striking instance of this occurred at a fire some
years since. It was a roaring gale of wind, and
the fire in a great building on Commercial Street.
When I got there a steamer was on each side of
the building throwing water upon the buildings on
the opposite side of the street. As the great
building, which was only on fire in one room in the

11

third story, became ignited in other rooms, lofts,
and the roof, the fire became tremendous, and
the heat drove the men guarding the opposite sides
so far apart, that their streams could not meet
by nearly a hundred feet; of course that was soon
on fire, which went rushing on down toward the
water. Again, on the opposite side of that fire
went down a hose from a steamer, and two men
holding the pipe kept the fire from the buildings
opposite. At that time I went home to Watertown, my clothes frozen stiff about me. If you
ask why I was so foolish, my answer is, that I
then knew that no people in the world were
fighting fire to PREVENT IT. And I was deter-
mined, if possible, to find out what would prevent
fires. While on West Boston Bridge, the attention of the passengers was called to the fact that
the fire was raging worse than ever. On arriving
home, I told my family that the fire had crossed
to the buildings on the wharf, and would go to
the water. But the morning paper said the fire
burnt to the water, and so up on the other side,
where it had destroyed 600,000 bushels of grain.
I told my friends that it was not so ; but that the
great fire we had seen on the bridge, had kept the
hosemen from going down on the opposite side of
the wharf, and so the fire crossed and went down
both sides at once. This was just what may have

been the cause of the fire catching at Otis Street. As what happened at that fire at the North End could occur wherever there was a high wind and great buildings, I looked to see if some other means could not have protected the two places, where the fire conquered the steam-engines. I saw, for I had such experience, that small engines in the opposite buildings, protected by the brick walls, and playing upon the wood-work of the windows and of the roofs, would be an ample protection for them, or that men by reaching out of the windows, their arms guarded by wetted cloth, and playing upon the wooden signs, the fire could have been kept on the other side of the street.

I called the attention of a number of Boston merchants to these facts; first, that such fires in a gale would rush right through the city, driving the steamers before them; and second, that small engines used in that manner would be sure to succeed, where others failed. Every one of them felt as I did; and one of them, I think Mr. George B. Upton, asked me to call upon Mr. Gardner Brewer, who he thought would be glad to see me, for he was quite interested upon the subject. He saw my idea in a moment. I said, " A fire may take west of this, and in a gale come down so wide that the steamers cannot throw their streams so that they may meet, and you have not the slightest protection." "Yes," said he, "and if the wind continues it will burn quite through the city." He requested me to call upon the chief engineer; and tell him that he and other merchants wished that some such method might be adopted. I knew that would be of no use, for the engineer did not know anything of organizing a new system; so I called on, and conversed with the committee on the fire department. Here again every one saw the idea, and again I was sent to the chief engineer. I saw him, and when I again saw the committee, their whole manner was changed. I knew in a moment what was the matter. I had been described as a " one idea man," by one who never had an idea; and so the whole thing was put back a generation. Some time after the great fire, I saw a communication in the "Boston Daily Advertiser," which gave me so much pleasure, filled as it was with common sense, that I inquired the name of the author, and was told that it was Mr. Gardner Brewer. I called upon him, although I supposed he had long forgotten me, and in the conversation he said, " I wrote a long communication to the city government in favor of your idea at that time, and from that day to this have received no answer."

Now I quote from the Fire Commission report: " Joseph Barnes, Fire Engineer of East Boston, witness. Question. Do you know how the fire got across Franklin Street? Answer. Yes, sir; I was there and saw the whole of it. Q. Where did it finally catch? A. It caught in the upper part of the buildings, on the Mansard roofs. By Mr. Greene: Q. That was Brewer's building? A. I think so. · Then it worked right up Franklin Street against the wind, etc. Q. Take that spot, Franklin Street, right across; suppose those roofs had not been Mansard, with the customary wooden trimmings, do you think the fire could have been stopped there? — And now comes the all-important answer. — A. Well, I think it rather doubtful. There was such intense heat that it was almost impossible to stand there. In the first of it, of course we stood over on the north side of Franklin Street, *but the heat came so heavy on us we had to back out each way, that is, down and up; I backed up toward Washington Street.*"

The same story. The heat was too great for the firemen to live in. They backed out, and the fire, which could have been arrested by small engines, protected from the fire by the thick walls, crossed to the opposite side, and the result was a loss of at least $25,000,000! Were the firemen at fault? No; the old city government, the old chief engineer, and the people of Boston, who elect men who know how to grind axes, to dine at Parker's, but not how to protect a city.

MISTAKES AT FIRES.

In the hurry and confusion attending the commencement of fires, mistakes are the easiest things in the world. The ten thousand people who assembled at the fire of November, before an alarm was given, and who did not give it themselves, made the first ten thousand. The firemen who did not get their hose up into the stores to play down upon the fire, made a great mistake. These were mistakes at the fire. But others of far greater importance were made. It was a mistake to have neglected to provide horses, when expressmen, coaches, omnibuses, and horse-cars had began to run, after the horse epidemic had almost ceased. But the great mistake of all was that of not having "two strings to one's bow." One kind of engine failed to reach the fire, and there was "no other string." Who that has read of great battles does not recollect that when bodies of infantry have been upon the point of giving way, they have been strengthened, and the tide of war turned, by the arrival of cavalry or batteries? And when batteries or cavalry have been just ready to give way, how often has a charge of a brigade of infantry sent the enemy away, stinging with the shame of defeat. So at the November fire. When the steam fire-engines failed to

throw water upon the Mansard roof which took
fire across the street from the first fire, there
should have been small engines taken up into
the garrets to protect them. They would have
been the infantry, to protect where the batteries
failed. " But," says a friend, " there were no
such small engines, which you call infantry, to do it
with." " True, my dear friend, there were none,
and that was the great mistake of the November
fire, and of the present fire-fighting system of this
country."

THE FIRE-ALARM TELEGRAPH.

That the fire-alarm is an excellent means of
calling the great engines to fires, is proved beyond
doubt, nor does there seem to be any fault found
with its management. If notice is not given at
the boxes it is the fault of others and not of those
at the office. But I wish to offer a suggestion,
which it has long seemed to me would add to its
practical usefulness. Many years ago I was in
the old town of Boston when there was a high
wind. I heard the town-crier, with his sonorous
voice, cry, "A great wind; look out for fire!"
The cry rang through the streets and was heard
in the houses and business portions of the town,
as he passed along. I thought then, and have ever
since, that it was an excellent idea, handed down

from the olden times; and now that it has for
many years been thrown aside, let me propose
that it should be taken up by the telegraph. At
the commencement of every hour, when there is a
dangerous wind, and at six P. M., when the business fires of the city are to be put out, let the telegraph give an alarm, which shall be understood to
say, " Take care of fire." Now, the first thing to
be heard about such a suggestion will be, it cannot
be done. True as preaching, if left to the great
army of can't-be-dones. If the telegraph opera-
tor, or the chief engineer, or the fire department
committee, or the Mayor, say so, then they, one
and all, are unfit for their places. It can be done,
and will not cost the city one cent of additional
expense, and it might some time save the whole
city from destruction by fire. There will be no
display, no show off, but the city will be more
secure from this dangerous enemy. " An ounce
of prevention is worth a pound of cure," and four
clangs from the telegraph may prevent a conflagration which would destroy a town or city. Don't
wait until the horse is stolen before you shut the
door.

WARNING SIGNALS.

In London, January, 1556, Alderman Christopher Draper employed a man to go about his
ward by night with a bell. After ringing it at

times he cried out, "Take care of your fires and lights; help the poor and pray for the dead." Hence arose the office of bellman in towns and cities. So, too, the old curfew bell is a corruption of the French *couvre feu* — fire-cover; for when it rang, it was a notice to all householders to shut the door of his house, cover up his fire, and get to bed. When the curfew was first rung, it was at seven o'clock; it was afterward changed to eight, and then to nine.

STEAM FIRE-ENGINES TO THROW STEAM INTO BUILDINGS.

It is very singular that this improvement has not been made in steam fire-engines. That a building on fire, but which has not burned "out" to the air, can be, if not too large, instantly extinguished, and with one tenth of the loss, especially if filled with merchandise, than it can be by water, is true beyond a doubt. Many of our great warehouses are so large that no one or perhaps two steamers could fill them, and thus they would not be saved in this manner, unless brick or iron walls are thrown across the buildings, as is the custom in Liverpool and London. I propose to describe the way the engines would be worked when this steam arrangement was made and the steamers altered so as to throw steam as well as water.

On arriving at a building on fire, the men would instantly perceive whether water or steam should be used; if water, the arrangement for work would go on as at present.   If the fire was confined within the building, the steam-pipe would be got ready, while one man, with the proper sized auger, bored a hole for the steam-pipe into some door or window near the fire.   That is all.   Water or steam.   Now one, then the other; and the property of the city vastly better protected by it, and at a very slight expense.   Steam has often been tried at different times; and as it has been under difficulties, it has often failed.   These failures were sure to have the widest circulation, while success has often been kept out of sight.   All buildings in which steam is used should be prepared so as to extinguish their own fires, which would save a great amount of property to the owners, and often to others.   Persons owning such buildings, and wishing to prepare them, may learn how simple the manner is by calling to see the kerosene works of the Downer Company at South Boston.   Of course such works, under the most careful direction, often take fire.   If a fire occurs there, in a minute the doors are shut, and steam turned into the building from the outside.   In from one to three minutes that portion of the buildings is crowded with steam, and the fire is out, when at its leisure the steam is allowed to escape, and the men go to their work again. One of the neighboring business men took quite an interest in this new way of getting rid of the dangerous element, and as the steam smothered out one fire after another, he became so excited as almost to wish that the fire would for once come off the conqueror. Hearing one day an unusual noise in that direction, he looked up and saw one of the buildings wholly enveloped in flames. " There!" said he, " now they will catch it!" and off he went, pell-mell, to get round to the front and witness the destruction. On his way he had to run a few rods out of sight of the fire. His last look showed no diminution of the flames, but when, after a run of ten rods, he turned into full view, the steam had been turned on, and to his unbounded astonishment, not the slightest sign of fire could be seen! He was as much taken aback as was the great dog with the locomotive, when it passed up and back on the Worcester railroad for the first time. A magnificent, old, and intelligent dog was kept within about twenty rods of the line of the railroad, and when the first engine went up, making, of course, as much noise as possible, the dog went for it. Rushing up to the bank under which the great machine was flying along at its fullest speed, he opened upon it his most furious bow-

wow-wow!—only to find that it was almost out
of sight away up the road. He stood a moment,
apparently thinking of the tremendous apparition,
and then slowly went back to his kennel. He
was observed to be nervous all the day, as if
something unusual was going on, 'and he must be
on the alert. In the afternoon down came the
locomotive with its one car, and doing its very
best to burst itself with screaming, and to get to
Boston a little ahead of no time, if possible. But
the dog was prepared for his twenty-rod race and
an attack on the new fiery enemy. Away went
the "screaming fire-devil," and away went the
furious, barking dog! When the four-footed animal looked over the bank there was nothing to be
seen, but turning his eyes eastward, he saw the
monster half-way down to where is now the All-
ston Station! "Mournfully and slow" went that
dog back to his home; and from that day, no
scream, rattle, crash, or roar which any train could
make, ever caused him to give a sign that he heard
it! So also the merchant "gave up," and let the
steam take care of the fires at Downer's at its
leisure! It would be very easy to bring about
this much-needed change, as when application was
made for using steam-power in a proper place, it
could be granted on condition that the parties
should introduce steam-pipes for extinguishing fires.

These would soon prove so efficient for that purpose, that all persons owning buildings using steam would find it for their interest to also introduce such pipes. There need be no fear that there will be too many ways to get rid of fires. It is because we have had but one string to our bow, *and that sometimes lost for fifteen or twenty minutes,* that we have so many fires at last culminating in the conflagration of November last.

GUNPOWDER TO AVERT CONFLAGRATIONS.

If upon this subject people only wrote or told what they knew, very little indeed would be written or said.

At the great fire of London, after two or three days of attempts to avert the flames by pulling down buildings, a resort was made to gunpowder, and with what success the following extracts will tell. Pepys says: "Now begins the practice of blowing up houses in Tower Street, those next the Tower, which at first did frighten the people more than anything; but it stopped the fire more than anything where it was done, it bringing down the houses to the ground in the same places they stood, and then it was easy to quench what little fire was in it, though it kindled nothing almost." This was Tuesday. Wednesday he says: "But going to the fire, I find, by the blowing up of

houses, and the great help given by the workmen
out of the king's yards, there is a good stop given
to it, as well at Mark Lane end as at ours." Evelyn, who was at the fire, thus describes it on Tuesday: " The burning still rages, and it was now got-
ten as far as the Inner Temple — all Fleet Street,
the Old Bailey, Ludgate Hill, Warwick Lane,
Newgate, Paul's Chain, Watling Street now flaming, and most of it reduced to ashes; the stones
of Paul's flew like granados, the melted lead running down the streets in a stream, and the very
pavements glowing with fiery redness, so as no
horse nor man was able to tread on them, and
the demolition had stopped all the water pipes, so
that no help could be applied. The eastern wind
still more impetuously drove the flames forward.
Nothing but the almighty power of God was able
to stop them, so vain was the help of man." Not
a word of gunpowder. He saw the fire in one
place and Pepys in another on Tuesday. Wednesday he says: " It crossed toward White Hall.
Oh, the confusion there was then in that court!
It pleased his Majesty to command me, among
the rest, to look after the quenching of Fetter
Lane end, to preserve, if possible, that part of
Holborn, while the rest of the gentlemen took
their posts (for they now began to bestir themselves, and not till now, who hitherto had stood,

as men intoxicated, with their hands across), and began to consider that nothing was likely to put a stop but the blowing up of so many houses as might make a wider gap than any had yet been made by the ordinary method of putting them down with the engines. This some stout seamen proposed early enough to have saved nearly the whole city, but this some tenacious and avaricious men, aldermen, etc., would not permit, because their houses must have been of the first. It was therefore now commanded to be practiced." . . . . And then he proceeds: "It now pleased God, by abating the wind, and by the industry of the people, that the fury of it began sensibly to abate about noon, so as it came no farther than the Temple westward, nor than the entrance of Smithfield north; but continued all this day and night towards Cripplegate and the Tower, as made us all despair." Another writer says: "After it had burnt three days and nights, some seamen taught the people to blow up the next houses with gunpowder, which stopped the fire." Burnet says: "All means used to stop it proved ineffectual, though the blowing up of houses was the most effectual of any."

Another says: "On that day (Tuesday) the houses near the Tower were blown up, and the same judicious plan was pursued in other places."

But we are also told that "the fire continued in the same excess all Monday, Tuesday, and Wednesday, until afternoon the fire decreased, having burned," etc. So we see how accounts differ, as they do and will, of all great fires and battles, each person telling the truth, from his point of view. The buildings blown up at the fire in London can, however, be no guide to people at fires in an American modern city. They were from twelve to eighteen feet high, with a very few and very small windows and doors. We, on the contrary, build them as high as "all out-doors," and make them up with one half of great windows. The blowing up of the buildings at Nantucket would have been no guide to the people of Boston, as there was not the least similarity between the two kinds of structures. The great question for the people of this country to solve is, How shall we erect our buildings and protect them by fire preventive, rather than by fire-fighting systems, so that we shall never be compelled to resort to untried methods by awful conflagrations? Let all the money for such purposes be expended in that direction by careful experiments, and my word for it, a hundred of the present rattle-trap buildings of the kind we now build will tumble down in the next century, where one will have to be blown up to arrest fire. It will be seen in this connection that granite suffered at the London fire, as well as at those of Chicago and Boston. Evelyn says, " the stones flew from Paul's like grenados."

If our American merchants will learn that it is better to acquire a name for strict integrity and honesty of purpose, rather than to show off flimsy goods, in great, scarecrow buildings, and our people will patronize them for it, rather than ape the follies of the worn-out families of Europe, we shall have more happy families, less " irregularities " in mercantile and family matters, and shall be more worthy the glorious independence which our fathers achieved for us, while their wives and children lived in buildings we have learned to despise.

HISTORY OF EXTINGUISHERS, ETC.

Many attempts have been made to discover some substance by which fires could be extinguished more readily than by water.

In 1734 a German physician invented balls of a composition, which, thrown into a fire, burst with violence and instantly quenched the fire.

In 1761 a composition of alum, sal-ammoniac, and other matters was invented and used for the same purpose. The same year Dr. Godfrey made successful experiments, and gunpowder was the motive for scattering the chemicals about the fire.

In 1792 a composition was made, by which two men and forty measures of the composition put out a fire that would have required twenty men and one thousand five hundred measures of water. The same year public experiments were made to prove that wood and similar matter might.be made incombustible by fire.

In 1794 Dr. Van Marum commenced experimenting, but found that he could extinguish more fire with water than with any other chemical which others had used or which he could find. In 1797 he prepared a building of dry wood, twenty-four feet in length, twenty-three wide, and fourteen high, with two doors on one side and two windows on the other. The inside of the building was thickly coated with pitch, and covered with twisted straw, wood shavings, and cotton soaked in turpentine. He says, " very soon after lighting it, the flames, being rendered more brisk by the wind, were everywhere so violent that it was considered as almost impossible to extinguish them." In a little more than four minutes it was extinguished with five buckets of water. The next experiment was more successful, three minutes and five gallons of water.

In 1792 an association of London architects reported that good party-walls were the best means for preventing the spread of fire from one building to another. From this we may suppose that party-walls which, from the fire of 1666 had so preserved the city, had been neglected, for their report was made in consequence of the " numerous fires." Directly following the report of the architects occurs the following remark : " Every fire, however large, must evidently have originated from a small beginning, and could doubtless have been prevented from assuming large and destructive proportions, were the means of checking its incipient mischief easily and quickly obtainable. Fires continually become destructive from delays in bringing the engines to the spot, from the want of water when they have got there, or delay in getting the engines to work." From this we see that the want of instant means of attacking fires has long been felt in England.

In 1797 Sir Samuel Bentham proposed placing tanks on the tops of buildings, connected with pipes laid all over the premises to be protected, and throughout the various floors, with provisions at various points for the attachment of hose and branch pipes, so that in case of a fire breaking out, the pressure on the tank would furnish an immediate and powerful jet at whatever point it might be needed. This plan is largely adopted in manufactories at the present day. In the workshops of the London and South Western Railway cast-iron pipes are perforated with small holes in the direction required, are laid along the roofs on the inside, and so arranged that each shop or portion supplied with these pipes can be put in connection with the water supply, and on turning a cock the pressure of the water drives it through the tubes and out at the various holes, deluging the whole area, with which they are in connection, and most effectually drowning out any fire that may have broken out, etc.

In 1812 Sir William Congreve patented a similar means of deluging all or any portion of a building with water.

In 1816 Captain Manby, of London, invented a portable apparatus, which was the origin of the present extinguisher. He made successful experiments with them, and they were brought to the notice of the insurance companies and refused, as a few years later was Ericsson and Braithwaite's splendid steam fire-engine. This engine was made every way in the same manner of the present fire extinguisher, and it was carried to the fire in a hand-cart containing six of them, or in a wagon, with horses. It was slung over the back when worked, and the contents, when mixed, threw themselves upon the fire. In the English work from which this account is taken is a notice of the great French invention, now called the " Extinguisher," to which it adds, " as brought out by Captain Manby, in 1816."

In 1820 it was proposed to furnish every house in London with a machine on wheels, containing ten gallons of water.

In 1828 salt was proposed as a preventive against fires, and reservoirs of brine were to be kept at various places.

The next experiment was with pearlash, which was said to be used at Liverpool and other places in England. I made an experiment with this in presence of some friends, according to the " book." I put out a fire with it surprisingly quick, and the hopes of the spectators were wonderfully raised. They were ready to cry Eureka. But the same kind of experiment was made next with water only, when, presto ! it was extinguished in half the time of the other. If a person had seen only the first experiment, and written an account for the papers, it would have been somewhat as follows : —

" Wonderful and important discovery ! An experiment was made yesterday with a new chemical for extinguishing fires. It worked in the most surprising manner, and a new era in protecting buildings may soon be introduced. We are not at liberty to reveal more at present, but the public may soon expect to hear that a complete change in the manner of extinguishing fires will be adopted," etc.

In 1855 Dr. Clanny gave, as a means for preventing a large fire, five ounces of ammonia and a gallon of water. The Chicago and Boston fires, being *very* large fires, would probably have required more of these substances, say a pound of ammonia and half a dozen gallons of water !

The extinguishers are excellent machines, and if they had been introduced truthfully, and with a regard to the safety of towns and cities, would perhaps have had a permanent place in the fire brigades of the world. But the first great error was, that they were said to put out tar, pitch, resin, oils, etc., while nothing else would do it.

From actual experiment, this has been proved to be incorrect. A water-engine, playing water only, and six or eight gallons of water per minute, will put out all the tar, pitch, resin, oils, or anything else which any extinguisher can, and as they would not cost one fourth as much, of course when distributed through a city, where they would be got to work so much sooner, would be sixteen times better.

Until the present time, no attempt has been made to have small engines or extinguishers distributed through a city, where they could be put to work in one minute, instead of fifteen, except for private protection. The result has been that at the dreadful conflagrations of Chicago and at Boston they were entirely ignored. They not only did no good at those fires, but at Chicago it is believed that more than a thousand of them were destroyed " unwept and unknown," and hundreds of them shared the same fate in Boston. They were purchased to protect the property of some one store or manufactory, but not to prevent fires anywhere else. But the fires started somewhere else, which could and should have been prevented, and grew into conflagrations, and the extinguishers were burned without so much as a notice in any accounts of the fires in either city. Their introduction into Boston, has been in accord with the tendency of the department to sacrifice efficiency to show.

First, half a dozen in a single wagon. Five minutes lost before they could be told of the fire, five more to get off, and ten at least before they could reach the fires on the average. Thus they would reach nine out of ten fires long after the steamers, which would have to drown out a small fire with a deluge of water, or wait until it had grown large enough to require a deluge, unless it was one of those slow mouldering fires which, if let alone, would be likely to go out of itself ! I venture to state that they have not yet put out one fire, which if there had been a system of large and small engines, once well at work, would not have been put out without an alarm, and with almost no loss at all. They are said to have been very useful at a fire at the north part of the city, where they saved a Catholic school after the fire had burned through its windows, etc. No doubt of that, and that perhaps if they had not been there just at the moment, the result would have been a conflagration. But with small engines there, the fire would never have got into the building at all. The little streams from the engines on the inside, directed back upon those windows, would have kept them and the building perfectly safe, while others of them could have probably dashed out the little fire when it was first seen and before an alarm was given, or held it in check until the arrival of the first steamer.

I was quite near the office of the "Old and New," when the alarm told that there was a fire in that building. I know how the steamers arrived before the extinguishers, how when they did arrive and went to work, one of the men came so near suffocation, as to prove that the steamers should have put out the fire rather than have waited for the fire to grow so large. I went into the building after the fire and made proper inquiries, and now I assert, that a Johnson pump, at any time for five minutes from the time the fire was first seen, would have put it out in a minute, and with not one hundredth part of the damage which was caused by waiting for the extinguishers.

The fire at Chandler's store, put out by an extinguisher in a minute or two, would have destroyed that store if the extinguisher had not been taken there from the neighboring store. Before the alarm could have been given, and the steamers got to work, the smoke would have been so dense that a stream could not have been got to the fire, which, as at the Winthrop House, would have gone all over the store destroying it at its leisure.

A small fire-engine would have done all which the extinguisher did, but in a few minutes more neither that, the extinguisher, or the steamers could have got within reach of the fire for the smoke in the building. Then the fire would have soon lighted up the streets, and there would have been a great battle, and the store and contents, about equally damaged by the fire and the water, would have been a total loss, and the next morning's papers would have gone over the old stereotyped story of the wonderful efficiency of the Boston Fire Department. All true as a fighting department, but a delusion, if we want a fire preventive system. An ounce of prevention is worth a pound of cure. Every few days we read that the extinguishers prevent a fire. But how small a part of the city they can protect. That is, to be near enough to know of the fire before the alarm is given. If they are better and cheaper than small water-engines, let it be known, and then have them placed so that they can be almost instantly used at every fire. Imitate the wisdom of all civilized nations, and by careful experiment, prove and know which are the best and most efficient, and then take the best for general use. "Prove all things. Hold fast to that which is good."

NEW FIRE PREVENTIVE METHOD.

About twenty years since a writer in the Boston papers, who had returned from Germany, gave an account of a kind of gymnast fireman who would mount to the roofs on the highest stories, without ladders and with great rapidity, and recommended that the same practice should be introduced into Boston for extinguishing fires. Young men were soon found who by practice could mount up on the outsides of buildings, but when they had got to the top of a building, they had no hose, nor buckets, nor engines; so when they had remained long enough in their pleasant situation, they imitated the king with forty thousand men who marched up a hill and then marched back again. They came down as wise as they went up, and the whole thing died away. And yet, out of that idea, so useless without engines, a most excellent and common-sense manner of preventing some kinds of fires may be organized. Suppose a fire in the second, third, or fourth story of a building is discovered, which has filled the rooms and entry up there with smoke, so that entrance cannot be got to it that way. Now suppose that there were distributed throughout the city a thousand iron ladders, with great hooks on the upper end to hook into the window where the fire is, and that there were kept with them a thousand engines with say twenty feet of hose. An engine could be taken into the loft below that on fire, and the hose taken up outside to the window and the pipe inserted in a few minutes, and thus many fires could be put out in a few minutes which, when the great engines had got to work, would have become so far advanced as to destroy the building and contents. Do not be afraid of having too many ways of getting rid of fires. We shall always have more of them than we want in this world.

FIRE AT THE TEMPLE HOUSE.

"At 10.20 o'clock this morning, word was brought to the Bulfinch Street engine-house that a fire was in progress at the Temple House in

Bowdoin Square, next the Revere. Without waiting for the horses, members of the Extinguisher
Steamer Four and the insurance companies seized
the Chemical Engine and drew it to the scene,
where a line of hose was taken into the fourth
story, and under the personal direction of the
chief, the fire was almost instantly extinguished
with an application of less than ten gallons of
water, although the quantity of carbonic acid gas
evolved was evidently great. The service rendered
by the Babcock in this instance was almost invalu-
able, for the time which would have been occupied
in getting an engine in service would have admitted a disastrous spread of the fire. As it is, the
damage will not exceed $100." The above extract is
from the Boston " Journal." In the " Globe " we
are told that " the chief engineer will probably recommend that four of these machines be purchased
for service in the fire department." Seeing these
notices in the papers, I went to the Temple
House to see about the fire. I knew the importance of having fire attacked at once, and was right
glad that the papers of Boston could at last tell
their readers, what I have so long endeavored to
get before the people, that " the time which would
have been occupied in getting an engine in service
would have admitted a disastrous spread of the
fire." The Gerrish Market, which was burned,

endangering a large part of the city, and the fire
in which, when first seen, was not two feet in
diameter; the Winthrop House and Masonic Temple, which the police reported could have been put
out with a few pails of water; the Fourth of July
fire, which, when first seen, could have been dashed
out with a bucket of water; the turret fire, which
could have been covered with a hat; and the hay
fire, which was, when first seen, only on one
bundle of hay, and could have been dumped into
the street in a minute, — these fires and many
others, I say, causing a loss of millions of dollars,
sufficiently prove this, and it is pleasant to know
that the people are to be taught it through the
press. But now let us see how Boston is to profit
by it. At the time of this Temple House fire.
which was very near the Babcock, every other
portion of the great city was left to the tender
mercies of the element of fire and the steamers,
"for the time which would have been occupied in
getting an engine in service would have admitted
a disastrous spread of the fire." Just so, exactly.
There was never a more important truth told.
The minutes lost between the time that the fire is
seen and that at which water is thrown upon it,
has, since the steam fire-engines have been in use,
cost millions of dollars before the great conflagration; and the $100,000,000 of that dreadful fire,

and the extra insurance in consequence of this
delay has, perhaps, been more than all the other
losses. Now, on this expensive fact an effort is
making to introduce another kind of engines, one
of which was so successful in putting out the fire
at the Temple House. I examined the fire there
this February 13, 1873, and I assert that, with
a Johnson pump, I, or any man of any experience,
could, if there had been just such a fire in each of
the four stories, have put them all out in five
minutes, — that is, so far as water was concerned!
With the "fire brigade" I have described in this
book for all hotels, the public would have never
known of the fire, for it would, with their "axe,
buckets, engine, and firemen" in the house, have
been out in five minutes, as it *would have been as
it was*, only that the firemen were just round the
corner, and could as well be called as not. We
are told that "the quantity of carbonic acid gas
evolved was evidently great." Do not the people
of Boston know enough to examine for themselves
and ascertain if water will not extinguish as much
fire as will an equal amount of that which is
thrown from the extinguishers, and at one fifth
the expense, when they are without carriage,
wheels, etc., or one twentieth of what it costs when
they have them? If not, let them engage a commission, the president of Harvard University, the

head of the Institute of Technology, and Professor
Horsford, or any other three men who are competent, and care for no especial system, but who would
be glad to have the city and the whole country
adopt the very best method of extinguishing fires.

Let us look a little closer into this. Twenty-
one of the "Babcock's" would cost forty-two
thousand dollars; and to work them a year, that
is, for horses, men, changes, etc., as much more,
or eighty-four thousand dollars. They could not
be got to work on an average, for they would seldom be called until the telegraph struck, in much
less than fifteen minutes; and supposing them
capable of extinguishing one hundred tar barrels
per minute, we should have a force of twenty-one
hundred of the barrels per minute. Now, for less
than fifty thousand dollars, we may have a force
of forty thousand barrels per minute, and one of
them at work in two minutes, and half a dozen, if
wanted, in three or four minutes, though one of
them would extinguish five out of six of all our
fires, if put to work in two minutes. And this is
not all. In at least a thousand of the most dangerous places in the city there would be "fire brigades" to be worked in a moment when a fire was
seen! The cost of the fire department — more than
$300,000 — and the dreadful fire of November,
show how serious the question is; and when a man

who has given so much attention to the subject as to enable him to understand it, tells you of the dangers, and you do not examine into it and adopt the best system, you will bitterly reap the consequences.

PORTABLE APPARATUS.

" We would earnestly recommend the general use of fire extinguishers and hand-pumps, in every building ; these would prevent many fires from becoming serious, and they would inspire confidence in cases of alarm of fire."— *Report of the Commissioners on the Fire.*

An experience of years with extinguishers and small engines, compels me to say, that few will get them, and the number will be much less who will attend to the detail and keep them in order. No doubt there were a thousand extinguishers destroyed by the fire in Chicago, and hundreds in the Boston fire ; yet one of them, or a little pump or two, would have prevented the Chicago fire, or prevented the spread of it to more than one building in Boston, if every portion of those cities had been protected by them.

The first question about a new means of protection should be, " Is it efficient ? " Of the small engines the answer is, " They will extinguish ten tar or resin barrels per minute each, or the number proposed for Boston, forty thousand barrels per minute." The next movement should be to so place them that every fire should be attacked long before the telegraph could even give an alarm. Do we not organize infantry, riflemen? What would be thought of a commission which should do away with these arms of defense, and should earnestly recommend the people to purchase them? It may serve to illustrate the manner of using them, to suppose them introduced in the following manner: Three thousand engines, ten regiments, and thirty companies. Each company would have its armory. This would cost many thousands of dollars, and then when the alarm-bell rang, all of the hundred men would run to the armory, take their engines and waiting for the word of command when all had arrived, they would be off double quick to the fire! Take another illustration. The police are kept in their different stations until a couple of drunken fellows get into a row. The people gather by thousands as now at fires, and at last the telegraph tells the men of the proper station of the row, and off they march with pistols and billies. Arrived upon the scene of action, the crowd is so great that it is impossible to reach and arrest the rioters, who now have increased by their several friends joining them to thousands; the billies and pistols would be used

13

upon the crowd, who after a time would run away
from this fusillade, *and most of the rioters with
them*, and the morning papers would report as follows: "Dreadful Riot! Last night there was a
dreadful riot in —— Street, and when the —— Police arrived they were obliged to fight their way into
the scene of bloody carnage, when they succeeded
in arresting six persons, who were so badly wounded
that they could not get away. The police were
obliged to carry them to the station in wagons.
We regret to say that no less than eight persons
were killed, and seventeen wounded, who were in
the crowd looking at the rioters." How does this
differ from the stereotyped account of fires, where
the "loss by water was far greater than by fire."
With a system of large and small machines, nine
times out of ten there would be neither loss by fire
or water. One day I had been showing a gentleman how efficient small engines would be, when
he observed, "Yes, every man should have one."
"But," said I, 'they won't do it." "Well," said
he, "they ought to, every man!" "But" said I,
"you know that every man should get religion,
which he can have without price, yet you know
that, according to your belief, not one in a hundred
does become a Christian; how then can you expect
that every person will purchase an engine to save
his house, if the engine costs ten dollars, when he

will not try to save his soul which he can do without price." He illustrated his idea by never paying a cent for an engine; and not long afterwards his place of business was destroyed, though the fire was seen when a small engine would have put it out in a minute if there, and his property, and that of others, would have been saved.

The small engines will need to be under supervision, and in their proper place in every building. The cost of this would be very small, a few thousand dollars per annum.

FIREMEN ALWAYS WORK NOBLY.

People never tire of praising the noble daring, and the earnestness which firemen display at their arduous and oftentimes dangerous work. With all this I fully sympathize. The Commission on the cause of the fire say, of the people who saved buildings on Oliver Street, at Hovey's store, and of the occupants of the buildings on the west side of Washington Street, who protected their buildings with wet cloths and carpets: " Similar efforts on the part of others would have saved property from destruction. . . . . The conduct of the gentlemen to whom we have referred as aiding the firemen by their personal exertions, was in marked contrast with the thoughtlessness of many spectators who crowded the streets, and greatly impeded

the efforts of the Department. In some cases violence was necessarily used toward these persons.
*Yet many of them would have gladly joined in
efforts to save property, if more well-directed efforts
had been made to that end.*"

Thank you, gentlemen. Here is the great truth
for the people to learn. The very thieves, the men
who stole and carried off the hundreds of thousands of dollars worth of property from the buildings on fire at Boston, had there been small engines there with which they could work, would
have kept the fire from these buildings, and have
done it with all their hearts, and have been better
men for it all their lives. Show any man how he
may protect the property of his neighbor from fire,
and he will work like a horse at an engine, pump-
ing or carrying water, as long as there is a hope
of success. The same men, with nothing to do,
will most of them stand in the way of the firemen,
and from them will drop out one, ten, or a hundred men, who, seeing that the goods will be
destroyed by fire, think they may as well have
them as to see them burned. All about that fire
there were places where small engines might have
been of the greatest service, and where, afterwards,
the steamers failed. At every such place there
were men enough to work the small engines. Do
you suppose that men who rushed into buildings

and perished while trying to save property, would not have worked at anything which would stay the progress of the fire? I have taken small engines to fires for many years, and I never saw a time when men and women, boys and girls, were not ready to aid me in my efforts at saving property. And I know, too, from pleasant experience, that young men who were fast becoming fire-rowdies, when they worked like heroes at a fire to save the homes of their neighbors, have changed and became likely, hopeful young men, and grown up good citizens. This is the tendency of helping at fires, — to make men better, more human, and civilized.

THE NEWTON FIRE DEPARTMENT.

This beautiful town, one of the most pleasantly located in the State, is divided into near a dozen pretty villages, interspersed by hills and valleys, some almost in a state of nature, while others are under the highest cultivation, and dotted over with the fine country homes of successful Boston merchants. In several of the villages there are steam fire-engines, in some of the others the old manual engine is used, and in two, at least, they have chemical engines. However inefficient the steamers may be for want of water, or for the distance from the fire, they are far better than the others, as they prevent the tendency to rowdyism, etc., which is almost sure to grow up were the others are used. Some months ago an alarm of fire was given in the village now called Newton, formerly Angier's Corner. No fire could be seen outside of the building said to be on fire, for many minutes. The fire was so small that it could have been dashed out in a minute by one of the Johnson, or other pumps invented by Newton men, in a minute. Even when the nearest steamer arrived, it could have been put out by either of the small pumps in a few minutes; but no such common-sense efficient means had been provided; and the steamer could not at once be got to work; and the fire, soon in the rooms and cellars filled with shavings and lumber, bid defiance to all the steamers, manuals, and chemicals which could be got together. So there was a great battle. All night, and even the next day, water was thrown upon the ruins. A few short comments, as an expert, I propose to offer upon this great battle. A ten-dollar engine — one of which should be within a minute of every part of the villages, in every such great building, and in every large, valuable private house in the town — would have extinguished that fire, and with less labor than was expended by the person who gave the alarm. The department saved the village. Yes, with the slight wind. But with a gale of wind blowing over the village the fire would have as certainly made its track through the village, as the neighboring Charles River follows its course to the sea, though it is to be hoped it would not have been as crooked as is that of the river.

The buildings of the town of Newton are not as safe from fire-danger since as before the fire, for the tendency of all such fire excitements is to make incendiaries, not directly out of the fire department, but from those who follow it, and glory in a fire as a place for fun and excitement.

Some time after this great fire, as the cars from Boston stopped at a depot near the Centre, the passengers saw a house in the neighborhood on fire. It was one of those sudden outbreaks which arise from grease, tar, or some similar substance on fire, and the house was threatened with speedy destruction. There were engines enough in town to put out a hundred such fires if they were there, and with water at hand. As it was, they might as well have been frozen up at the north pole. For a moment the passengers let the fire burn on. Then one of them, catching a pail or something, exclaimed, "Let us put out the fire," and at it he went, followed by a dozen others. Such work almost always is successful, and in a few minutes they had driven the fire out of the house, and were on their way home, happy in the consciousness of doing something to save the property of their

neighbors, better firemen, and so better members
of society. There was more than ten times as
much fire and danger at this fire, which was put
out by a few men with pots, kettles, and a pail
or two, than there was for several minutes at the
fire which, neglected at Newton, became so great
a fire and kept the department at work all night,
and caused the out-of-town steamers to be sent
for. Now if the town of Newton will purchase
and distribute small engines about the town (for
they are vastly better than pails and dippers
alone), at an expense which one steam fire-engine,
land, house, horses, etc., and the pay of the engine-
men for one year will cost, and distribute cards of ·
directions for the people, so that they may know
how to work them, the small engines will extinguish
nine out of ten of all the fires which will be in
the town for the next ten years. Delay makes the
danger. How often have the engines of the town,
when an alarm has been given, gone rushing off
miles to fight a fire which had so far gone over a
building as to render it of no possible value. How
often has the result been " total loss." How seldom " the engine extinguished the fire with a loss
of a few dollars." I know when I see such accounts that it is the system and not the firemen
who are at fault; but I want the system changed,
that the good people of Newton, and of the State,

the United States, aye, the world, may rest secure from great fires and conflagrations.

EDUCATION FOR FIREMEN.

" 'Tis education forms the common mind, —
Just as the twig is bent, the tree's inclined."

" The firemen are drilled first daily, and then three times a week for some months, and this with an average of three calls a day soon makes them acquainted with the routine of their business ; but it takes years of constant work, to make a thoroughly good fireman." So says James Braidwood, speaking of the men of the London Fire Brigade.

I propose that every boy and girl who graduates from a grammar school in the United States, should be an educated fireman or firewoman. Not like those of the London Brigade, but that they should know how at once to attack fires, and with the knowledge and means which would almost always insure success. It was my pleasure some years since to have conversations with a former President of Harvard University upon this subject of fires. He also taught his children what to do if a fire occurred on the premises. One of the boys when in college woke up one night, and found the outer room of his suite on fire. The thermometer was below zero, the water-pipes were frozen up, and the nearest water was to be had at a pump quite a distance from the building. He had bathed the night before and that water had not been thrown away. By using it with care, a little water just where it was wanted, there was enough to extinguish the fire. In the mean time the fire had been seen by a watchman, who gave an alarm which brought out all the fire department. So much for an education which now cannot be acquired in any school in the country. While thinking of the ex-president, I will write an anecdote he told me, for I think it may be of great use to any person who does not know of the practical way of extinguishing fires which it illustrates.

When a lad he sometimes worked in a cabinet-maker's shop. One day he helped the workmen make up part of a barrel of varnish. In the evening when the owner came home and was looking about the place, he saw the varnish barrel. To satisfy his curiosity, he took out the bung, and looked into the barrel, and to aid his vision he held the light near the bung-hole, when presto! the vapor from the barrel met the blaze of the lamp, and ran back into the barrel; the varnish took fire, and in two hours the great shop, sheds, stock, furniture, and I think the house and barn, were in ashes. Now for the lesson. "If," said the President, "the man had clapped his hand instantly upon the bung-hole, or put the bung in, or, if too hot, he had seized a rag or a piece of board, and covered it, the fire would have been out in a moment." Asking my readers to remember this, I pass to my lesson upon the education of firemen.

Every grammar-school teacher should be able to tell of the danger of spontaneous combustion, of each new chemical as it is discovered, of the danger of friction matches, oils, etc., and how to avoid the danger if they set fire to a house, or to the clothing on a person. They should also have at the school an engine, with which they should at special times experiment before the highest class, both of boys and girls, and should also have a hatchet or an axe, or both, and explain how fire may now work its way over a building between the walls of the ceiling or partitions, and that the walls can easily be broken by an axe or hatchet, when water enough to put out the fire may be thrown into such places with the engine. They should be taught that water will put out kerosene, tar, resin, and similar substances which may have taken fire about the house, and above all, they should teach the value of a calm, collected, fearless, and earnest method of attacking fire and of meeting any danger.

This should be also taught to the pupils of all the State and city Normal Schools, and experiments made with small fires, to show how very effective such means are when early applied, to put out even fires of considerable magnitude, and which would insure the destruction of buildings a few minutes later.

All this should be done with the decorum and dignity which a subject so solemn as the destruction of our homes, often all our earthly possessions, is entitled to. I mention this because I am sorry to say that a large portion of our boys and young men have been taught that the great use of an engine is to play more or farther than another, while the safety of the community is a matter of secondary importance. Therefore the appearance of a fire-engine in the streets is a signal for fun and jollity. It should no more be so, than should be a small-pox ambulance. Children and young people who go to fires for fun, also acquire bad manners and habits, and soon become immoral; while the youth taught how to be useful at fires goes home a better and more thoughtful person for having in some way been instrumental in saving the building of a neighbor from destruction. I have known many young persons ruined soul and body by running with engines, and I have also known others who have helped me, while fighting fires, grow up thoughtful men. I am sure that each of these two tendencies is certain. The one tending downwards, and the other upwards. Teaching this would make our homes more safe, and our children would be, growing under such influence, better, more easily governed, and more likely to make intelligent and useful citizens in the community. In all this avoid using any kind of engines which are set upon wheels to be run to fires. The devil has no such aid as that. More young men have gone out of our schools, good and virtuous to be made over into roughs and black-guards in this way than any other that I know of in our country.

Experiments should be made with extinguishers and small engines, without wheels. This will at once show by practical experience that for pro-tecting a whole village, town, or city from fire, the small engine is so much cheaper than the other that the same money appropriated for the engines would make the place at least ten times more efficient than by the purchase of extinguishers. I most earnestly and respectfully ask our Educators, our Board of Education, their Secretary, Presidents of Colleges, and the School Committees of the towns in the State to give this subject their most serious attention, as I believe it is of great impor-tance, as it would make the property of the com-munity more safe, and be a means for the moral improvement of young people. It is delightful to sing, and all who have the capacity, should learn to sing, but the most heartfelt song of thanksgiving we think, would come from a family whose house had been preserved from destruction by fire, through the knowledge their children had acquired in school upon that important subject, THE BEST MANNER OF INSTANTLY EXTINGUISHING FIRES.

CHAPTER X.

HISTORIC FIRES.

As we refer back to some great storm, earthquake, or other convulsion of nature, as data by which to recall events, or to compare with events of a similar kind, so for more than two hundred years

THE GREAT FIRE OF LONDON

has been the measure by which historians have compared the fires of other times, and all of them falling far below it, until the dreadful conflagration of Chicago.

All, however, which is known about that awful fire, except to a few readers, is that it burned a great portion of the city, and that it ended the desolation which the plague brought upon the city. Its lessons of caution, as regards the proper manner of building and of the means of preventing fires, cannot but be useful to all who will study them; and as there were persons who were at the fire, and who wrote excellent descriptions of it, which enable us to compare it with the conflagrations of Chicago and of Boston, it can hardly fail to be interesting to the general reader : —

" This dreadful and deplorable fire broke out in
the dead time of Saturday night in the house of Mr.
Farryner, a baker, in Pudding Lane, when the eyes
and senses of all were locked up in sleep. The
house was a wooden building, pitched on the outside, as all the rest in the lane were; the lane
too exceeding narrow, and, by the jutting over of
the several stories, the houses on each side almost
met at top. Add to these, that the house in
which the fire began being full of brush and fag-
got wood, the fire soon got to a head, and furiously
seized on the neighboring houses on all sides, running four ways at once. It fell upon the Star Inn,
then full of hay and straw; whence communicating
its fury to New Fish Street, it set all on a flame.
And another branch raging down the lane, laid
hold on Thames Street, the repository of all combustibles, as butter, cheese, wine, brandy, sugar,
oil, hemp, flax, resin, pitch, tar, brimstone, cordage, hops, wood, and coals; where, redividing itself,
it ran both eastward and westward with a fury
inexpressible, and attacking the adjacent lanes,
committed the most deplorable ravages; and its
two main branches meeting at London Bridge,
soon reduced all the buildings thereon, together
with the water machines under the same, whereby
they were at once deprived of the assistance of
that element (the new river water not being then

laid into those parts), whereupon it immediately got to such a head as to triumph over all means whatsoever.

" As it happened on Saturday night, and in the dead of the vacation, a vast number of the principal citizens were in the country either about business or pleasure, and their houses left in the care of servants, took off a great number of hands that otherwise would have been of great service in helping to extinguish the flames.

" The spring and summer had been the driest in the memory of man, whereby the houses, which were all built of wood, without party-walls, were prepared, as it were, for fuel for this terrible conflagration.

" At the breaking out of the fire a violent east wind blew ; which continuing to rage for the space of three days, it drove the flames with such an excessive rapidity, that, considering the nature of the buildings, it was of itself sufficient, without the help of villainy, to reduce the city to a chaos.

" After this dreadful and destructive fire had for three days raged with the utmost violence, and seemingly in contempt of all means used to extinguish the same, it was at last, by the ceasing of the wind, conquered ; after it had laid waste and consumed the buildings on four hundred and thirty-six acres of ground, four hundred streets, lanes, etc.,

14

thirteen thousand two hundred houses, the cathedral church of St. Paul, eighty-six parish churches, six chapels, the magnificent buildings of Guildhall, the Royal Exchange, Custom-house, and Blackwell Hall, divers hospitals and libraries, fifty-two of the companies halls, and a vast number of other stately edifices, together with three of the city gates, four stone bridges, and the prisons of Newgate, the Fleet, the Poultry and Wood Street compters; the loss of which, together with that of merchandise and household furniture, by the best calculation, amounted to ten millions seven hundred and thirty thousand and five hundred pounds. Yet, notwithstanding this terrible devastation, only six persons lost their lives thereby.

" Whatever the unfortunate citizens of London suffered by the late dreadful fire, 'tis manifest, that a greater blessing could not have happened for the good of posterity; for, instead of very crooked, narrow, and incommodious streets (fitter for a wheelbarrow than any nobler carriage), dark, irregular, and ill-contrived wooden houses, with their several stories jutting out, or hanging over each other, whereby the circulation of the air was obstructed, noisome vapors harbored, and verminous, pestilential atoms nourished, as is manifest by this city's not being clear of the plague for twenty-five years before, and only free from contagion for

three years in above seventy. But, since the en-
largement of the streets, and modern way of building, by the reëdifying of London, there is such a
free circulation of sweet air through the streets,
that offensive vapors are expelled, and the city
freed from pestilential symptoms for these eighty-
nine years." — *From Maitland's " History of
London."*

Burnet says : " The summer had been the driest that was known of some years. And London
being for the most part built of timber filled
up with plaster, all was extreme dry. On the
second of September a fire broke out, that raged for
three days, as if it had a commission to devour
everything that was in its way. On the fourth it
stopt, in the midst of very combustible matter."
Another writer says: " The magistrates of the
city assembled quickly together, and with the
usual remedies of buckets, which they were provided with. But the fire was too ravenous to be
extinguished with such quantities of water as those
instruments could apply to it, and fastened still
upon new material before it had destroyed the old.
And though it raged furiously all that day, to that
degree that all men stood amazed, as spectators
only, no man knowing what remedy to apply, nor
the magistrates what orders to give: yet it kept
within some compass," etc.

" But in the night the wind changed and carried the danger from thence, but with so great and irresistible violence, that as it kept the English and Dutch fleets from grappling, when they were so near each other, so it scattered the fire from pursuing the line it was in with all its force, and spread it over the city: so that they who went late to bed at a great distance from any place where the fire prevailed, were awakened before morning with their own house's being in a flame; and whilst endeavor was used to quench that, other houses were discovered to be burning, which were near no place from whence they could imagine the fire could come," etc.

The fire was flying over the heads of the spectators and setting new fires, to burn together into one conflagration.

" The fire and the wind continued in the same excess all Monday, Tuesday, and Wednesday, till afternoon, and flung and scattered brands burning into all quarters; the nights more terrible than the days, and the light the same, the light of the fire supplying that of the sun. And indeed whoever was an eye-witness of that terrible prospect, can never have so lively an image of the last conflagration till he beholds it."

The following testimony in favor of brick buildings is from the same writer: " It was observed that where the fire prevailed most, when it met with brick buildings, if it was not repulsed, it was so well resisted that it made a much slower progress; and when it had done its worst, that the timber and all the combustible matter fell, it fell down to the bottom within the house, and the walls stood and inclosed the fire, and it was burned out without making a further progress in many of those places; and then the vacancy so interrupted the fury of it, that many times the two or three next houses stood without much damage."

The people of London, as at Chicago and Boston, and as they will at all such conflagrations, believed that the city was set on fire. The following extract will give a sufficient reason for this one : " There was never any probable evidence that there was any other cause of that woeful fire than the displeasure of God Almighty. The first accident of the beginning in a baker's house, where there was so great a stock of faggots, and the neighborhood of much combustible matter of pitch and resin and the like, led it in an instant from house to house to Thames Street, with the agitation of so terrible a wind to scatter and disperse it." A very instructive and interesting lesson may be learned from the following account of the saving of a great amount of stationers' goods and their loss afterwards. The loss of the stationers was £200,000. "All those who dwelt near Paul's carried their goods, books, paper, and the like, as others of greater trades did their commodities, into the large vaults which were under St. Paul's Church, before the fire came thither: which vaults, though all the church above the ground was afterwards burned, with all the houses round about, still stood firm and supported the foundation, and preserved all that was within them ; until the impatience of those who had lost their houses, and whatsoever they had else, in the fire, made them very desirous to see what they had saved, upon which all their hopes were founded to repair the rest. It was the fourth day after the fire ceased to flame, though it still burned in the ruins, from whence there was still an intolerable heat, when the booksellers, especially, and some other tradesmen, who had deposited all they had preserved in the greatest and most spacious vault, came to behold all their wealth, which to that moment was safe ; but the doors were no sooner opened, and the air from without fanned the strong heat within, but the driest and most combustible matters broke into a flame, which consumed all, of what kind soever, that till then had been unhurt there. Yet they who had committed their goods to some lesser vaults, at a distance from that greater, had better fortune ; and having learned from the second ruin of their friends to have more patience, attended till the rain fell, and extinguished the fire in all places, and cooled the air : and then they securely opened the doors, and received all from thence that they had there."

The following extracts from the diary of Sir John Evelyn, describing this fire, are of great value, as he was a good writer, and he had foretold the danger unless more care was used in the disposition of the more dangerous substances about the city. He also drew a plan for rebuilding the city, which would have been a great improvement, but it was rejected, as was that of Sir Christopher Wren.

Sept. 3d. " The fire continuing, after dinner I took coach with my wife and son and went to the Bankside in Southwark, where we beheld that dismal spectacle, the whole city in dreadful flames near the water side; all the houses from the bridge, all Thames Street, and upwards towards Cheapside, down to the Three Cranes, were now consumed. . . . . The fire having continued all this night (if I may call that night which was light as day for ten miles round about, after a dreadful manner) when conspiring with a fierce eastern wind in a very dry season; I went on foot to the same place, and saw the whole south part of the city burning from Cheapside to the Thames, and all along Cornhill (for it likewise kindled back against the wind as well as forward), Tower Street, Fenchurch Street, Gracious Street, and so along to Brainard's Castle, and was now taking hold of St. Paul's Church, to which the scaffolds contributed exceedingly. The conflagration was so universal, and the people so astonished, that from the beginning, I know not by what despondency or fate, they hardly stirred to quench it, so that there was nothing heard or seen but crying out and lamentation, running about like distracted creatures without at all attempting to save even their goods; such a strange consternation there was upon them, so as it burned both in breadth and length, the churches, public halls, Exchange, hospitals, monuments, and ornaments, leaping after a prodigious manner, from house to house and street to street, at great distances one from the other; for the heat with a long set of fair and warm weather, had even ignited the air and prepared the materials to conceive the fire, which devoured after an incredible manner houses, furniture, and everything. Here we saw the Thames covered with goods floating, all the barges and boats laden with what some had time and courage to save, as, on the other, the carts, etc., carrying out to the fields, which for many miles were strewed with movables of all sorts, and tents erecting to shelter both people and what goods they could get away. Oh the miserable and calamitous spectacle! such as haply the world had not seen since the foundation of it, nor be outdone till the universal conflagration thereof."

This little piece of prophecy, which tends to show how much larger was the Chicago fire than that of London, calls to my mind another which occurred soon after the settlement of Boston and vicinity. The Assembly gave a committee of persons instructions to build a road from the settled portion of Watertown (near the mill) to that portion of it west, now Waltham, and so toward Weston. The committee no doubt made an excellent road, and so reported; and had they concluded their report there, all would have been well, but some persons can never stop when they have told their tale, and so they added, "and we suppose there will never be wanted a road any farther westward!" But to the fire. "All the sky was of a fiery aspect, like the top of a burning oven, the light seen above forty miles round about for many nights. God grant mine eyes may never behold the like, who now saw above 10,000 houses all in one flame." This will be better understood when I say that the roofs of many houses were covered with pitch, and burned with great fury and rapidity, while in the narrow streets and lanes, almost all the houses were made of timber, like the log-huts of new countries, which burned slowly, but with an intense heat for days. There were hundreds of acres of this terrible heated, slow fire, and on the outside the on-rushing fire, catching upon the buildings not yet burned. At Chicago, the fire burned out almost as fast as it ran forward; especially was this true of the west and north divisions. It was also true to some extent at the Boston fire. If the buildings had burned as long and as intensely at Boston as at London, when the fire was arrested upon the outside lines, there would have been about sixty acres of solid fire on the ground which had been burnt over. "The noise and crashing and thunder of the impetuous flames, the shrieking of women and children, the hurry of people, the fall of towers, houses, and churches, was like an hideous storm, and the air all about so hot and inflamed that at the last one was not able to approach it, so that they were forced to stand still, and let the flames burn on, which they did for near two miles in length, and one in breadth. The clouds also of smoke were dismal, and reached upon computation near fifty miles in length. Thus I left it this afternoon burning, a resemblance of Sodom, or the last day. . . . London was, but is no more."

They were " forced to stand still and let the flames burn on." The only means for throwing water upon the fire were buckets (for the *en-*

gines were only the fire-hooks for pulling down buildings); and it will be at once seen that while water could only be thrown from them ten or twelve feet, the heat of the terrible fire, when it had spread over many acres, would prevent those working with buckets from approaching within an hundred feet of the fire. The heat of the Chicago and Boston fires, from the height of the buildings, was so great in many places, that the firemen with their great steamers could not approach near enough to throw water with any effect into the fire or on the stores which were catching upon the outside.

On the fourth he writes: "The burning still rages, and it was now gotton as far as the Inner Temple, all Fleet Street, the Old Bailey, Ludgate Hill, Warwick Lane, Newgate, Paul's Chain, Watling Street now flaming, and now most of it reduced to ashes; the stones of St. Paul's flew like granados, the melting lead running down the streets in a stream, and the very pavements glowing with fiery redness, so as no horse nor man was able to tread on them, and the demolition had stopped all the passages, so that no help could be applied. The eastern wind still more impetuously driving the flames forward. Nothing but the almighty power of God was able to stop them, for vain was the help of man."

Sept. 5th. "It crossed towards Whitehall; but oh, the confusion there was then at that court! It pleased his Majesty to command me among the rest to look after the quenching of Fetter Lane end, to preserve if possible that part of Holborn, whilst the rest of the gentlemen took their several posts, some at one part, some at another (for now they began to bestir themselves, and not till now, who hitherto had stood as men intoxicated, with their hands across) and began to consider that nothing was likely to put a stop but the blowing up of so many houses as might make a wider gap than any had yet been made by the ordinary method of pulling them down with engines; this some stout seamen proposed early enough to have saved near the whole city, but this some tenacious and avaricious men, aldermen, etc., would not permit, because their houses must have been of the first. It was therefore now commanded to be practiced, and my concern being particularly for the Hospital of St. Bartholomew near Smithfield, where I had many wounded and sick men, made me more diligent to promote it; nor was my care for the Savoy less. It now pleased God by abating the wind, and by the industry of the people, when almost all was lost, infusing a new spirit into them, that the fury of it began sensibly to abate about noon, so as it came no farther than the Temple westward, nor than the entrance of Smithfield north; but continued all this day and night so impetuous towards Cripplegate and the Tower as made us all despair; it also broke out again in the Temple, but the courage of the multitude persisting, and many houses being blown up, such gaps and desolations were soon made, as with the former three days' consumption *the back fire did not so vehemently urge upon the rest as formerly. There was yet no standing near the burning and glowing ruins by near a furlong's space."* So we see, the heat was too great for persons to approach the great mass of ruins within near forty rods !

This is what he had written to his Majesty: " The coal and wood wharfs and magazines of oil, resin, etc., did infinite mischief, so as the invective which a little before I had dedicated to his Majesty, and published, giving warning what might probably be the issue of suffering those shops to be in the city, was looked on as a prophecy. The poor inhabitants were dispersed about St. George's Fields, and Moorfields, as far as Highgate, and several miles in circle, some under tents, and some under miserable huts and hovels, many without a rag or any necessary utensils, bed or board, who from delicateness, riches, and easy accommodations, in stately and well furnished houses, were now reduced to extremest misery and poverty. In this calamitous condition I returned with a sad heart to my house, blessing and adoring the distinguishing mercy of God to me and mine, who in the midst of all this ruin was like Lot, in my little Zoar, safe and sound."

Sept. 7th. " I went this morning on foot from Whitehall, as far as London Bridge, through the late Fleet Street, Ludgate Hill, by St. Paul's, Cheapside, Exchange, Bishopsgate, Aldersgate, and out to Moorfields, thence through Cornhill, etc., with extraordinary difficulty, clambering over heaps of yet smoking rubbish, and frequently mistaking where I was. The ground under my feet so hot, that it even burnt the soles of my shoes. In the mean time his Majesty got to the Tower by water, to demolish the houses about the graff [the ditch or moat], which being built entirely about it, had they taken fire and attacked the White Tower where the magazine of powder lay, would undoubtedly not only have beaten down and destroyed all the bridge, but sunk and torn the vessels in the river, and rendered the demolition beyond all expression for several miles about the country." On his return one would suppose he passed through the ruins of Boston or Chicago. " At my return I was infinitely concerned to find that goodly Church of St. Paul's now a sad ruin, and that

beautiful portico (for structure comparable to any
in Europe, as not long before repaired by the late
King), now rent in pieces, *flakes of vast stone split
asunder*, and nothing remaining entire but the inscription in the architrave, showing by whom it
was built, which had not one letter of it defaced.
It was astonishing to see what immense stones
the heat had in a manner calcined, so that all the
ornaments, columns, friezes, and projectures of
massy Portland stone flew off, even to the very
roof, where a sheet of lead covering a great space
. . . . was totally melted," etc. . . . . . "Nor yet
was I able to pass through any of the narrower
streets, but kept the widest; the ground and air,
smoke and fiery vapor, continued so intense that
my hair was almost singed, and my feet unsuffer-
ably surheated. The by-lanes and narrower streets
were filled up with rubbish, nor could one possibly
have known where he was, but by the ruins of
some church or hall, that had some remarkable
tower or pinnacle remaining. I then went towards
Islington and Highgate, where one might have seen
two hundred thousand people of all ranks and de-
grees dispersed and lying along by their heaps of
what they could save from the fire, deploring their
loss, and though ready to perish for hunger and destitution, yet not asking one penny for relief, which
to me appeared a stranger sight than any I had yet

beheld. His Majesty and Council indeed took all imaginable care for their relief by proclamation for the country to come in and refresh them with provisions. In the midst of all this calamity and confusion, there was, I know not how, an alarm begun that the French and Dutch, with whom we were now in hostility, were not only landed, but even entering the city. There was in truth some days before great suspicion of those two nations joining; and now, that they have been the occasion of firing the town. This report did so terrify, that on a sudden there was such an uproar and tumult that they ran from their goods, and taking what weapons they could come at, they could not be stopped from falling on some of those nations whom they casually met, without sense or reason. The clamor and peril grew so excessive that it made the whole Court amazed, and they did with infinite pains and great difficulty reduce and appease the people, sending troops of soldiers and guards to cause them to retire into the fields again, where they were watched all this night. I left them pretty quiet, and came home sufficiently weary and broken. Their spirits thus a little calmed, and the afright abated, they now began to repair into the suburbs about the city, where such as had friends or opportunity got shelter for the present, to which his Majesty's proclamation also invited them."

And now for Pepys's "Diary," the man who
ells of everything; most of which carries us so
ear the fire that we almost feel the heat, and
over our faces from the smoke, ride with him on
he river, eat or drink with him at home or at the
eer-shops, visit the king; in short, we learn all
bout the fire, and almost everything else, in or
ut of his family.

"*September 2, Lord's Day.* Some of our
maids sitting up late last night to get things
eady for our feast to-day. Jane called us up
bout three in the morning, to tell us of a great
ire they saw in the City, so I rose and slipped on
my night-gown, and went to her window; and
hought it to be on the back side of Mark Lane at
he farthest, but being unused to such fires as fol-
owed, I thought it far enough off; and so went
o bed again, and to sleep. About seven rose again
o dress myself, and there looked out at the win-
low, and saw the fire not so much as it was, and
arther off. So to my closet to set things to rights,
fter yesterday's cleaning. By and by Jane comes
nd tells me that she hears that above three hun-
lred houses have been burned down to-night by
he fire we saw, and that it is now burning down
ll Fish Street, by London Bridge. So I made
myself ready presently and walked to the Tower,
nd there got up upon one of the high places, Sir

J. Robinson's little son going up with me; and there I did see the houses at that end of the bridge all on fire, and an infinite great fire on this and the other side the end of the bridge; which, among other people did trouble me for poor little Michell and our Sarah on the bridge. So down with my heart full of trouble to the Lieutenant of the Tower, who tells me that it begun this morning in the King's baker's house [his name was Faryner], in Pudding Lane, and that it hath burned down to St. Magnes Church and most part of Fish Street already. So I down to the water side, and there got a boat, and through bridge, and there saw a lamentable fire. Poor Michell's house, as far as the Old Swan, already burned that way, and the fire running farther, that in a very little time it got as far as the Steel Yard, while I was there. Everybody endeavoring to remove their goods, and flinging into the river, or bringing them into lighters that lay off; poor people staying in their houses as long as till the very fire touched them, and then running into boats or clambering from one pair of stairs by the water side to another. And among other things, the poor pigeons, I perceive, were loth to leave their houses, but hovered about the windows and balconies till they burned their wings, and fell down. Having stayed and in an hour's time

een, the fire rage every way, and nobody, to my
ight, endeavoring to quench it, but to remove
heir goods, and leave all to the fire, and having
een it gét as far as the Steel Yard, and the wind
aighty high, and driving it into the City; and
verything after so long a drought proving com-
ustible, even the very stones of churches, and
mong other things the poor steeple [St. Law-
ence Poultney], by which pretty Mrs. ——
ives, and whereof my old schoolfellow Elborough
3 parson, taken fire in the very top, and there
urned till it fell down: I to Whitehall (with
l gentleman with me, who desired to go off from
he Tower, to see the fire, in my boat); and there
ip to the King's closet in the Chapel, where peo-
le come about me, and I did give them an ac-
ount dismayed them all, and word was carried
n to the King. So I was called for, and did tell
he King and Duke of York what I saw, and that
inless his Majesty did command houses to be
ulled down, nothing could stop the fire. They
eemed much troubled, and the King commanded
ne to go to my Lord Mayor [Sir Thomas Blud-
vorth] from him, and command him to spare no
iouses, but to pull down before the fire every way.
Che Duke of York bid me tell him, that if he
vould have any more soldiers, he shall; and so
lid my Lord Arlington afterwards. as a oreat

secret. Here meeting with Capt. Cocke, I in his
coach, which he lent me, and Creed with me to
Paul's, and there walked along Watling Street,
as well as I could, every creature coming away
loaden with goods to save, and here and there
sick people carried away in beds. Extraordinary
good goods carried in carts and on backs. At
last met my Lord Mayor in Canning Street, like
a man spent, with a handkercher about his neck.
To the King's message, he cried, like a fainting
woman, 'Lord, what can I do? I am spent;
people will not obey me. I have been pulling
down houses; but the fire overtakes us faster
than we can do it.' That he needed no more soldiers; and that for himself, he must go and refresh himself, having been up all night. So he left
me, and I him, and walked home; seeing people
almost distracted, and no manner of means used
to quench the fire. The houses too so very thick
thereabouts, and full of matter for burning, as
pitch and tar, in Thames Street; and warehouses of oil, and wines, and brandy, and other
things." Much has been said of the inefficiency
of the Mayor at this fire. But let us look at the
facts, just where Pepys gave him the command of
the king to pull down buildings. Hundreds of
buildings must have been on fire, burning in every
direction, and there were no means of throwing

vater except from buckets, and the engines for
)ulling down buildings were small and wholly
mfit to pull down the heavy timber buildings.
3esides, the people were under no officers, and the
Mayor, the only fire officer, was not a fire officer at
.ll. The fire must have been so hot that no per-
on could have gone near enough to throw water
ipon it, and it had become a conflagration; and the
Mayor, when asking men to do what he and every
)ne could see would be of no use, and who could
)ossibly save a few valuables from their burning
houses, might well exclaim, "People will not obey
ne." No, the city must have and ought to have
)een destroyed, a warning to all people to invent
neans to protect a city from fire. No man living,
hen or since, could have saved it with the means
ie had at his command. But to return to the
' Diary ": "Here I saw Mr. Isaac Houblon, the
iandsome man, prettily dressed and dirty, at his
loor at Dowgate, receiving some of his brother's
hings, whose houses were on fire; and, as he says,
iave been removed twice already; and he doubts
(as it soon proved) that they must be in a little
ime removed from his house also, which was a sad
onsideration. And to see the churches all filling
vith goods by people, who themselves should be
[uietly there at this time. By this time it was
hout twelve o'clock; and so home, and there find

my guests, who were Mr. Wood and his wife Bar-
bary Shelden, and also Mr. Moone: she mighty
fine, and her husband, for aught I see, a likely
man. . . . . Soon as dined, I and Moone away,
and walked through the City, the streets full of
nothing but people, and horses and carts loaden
with goods, ready to run over one another, and
removing goods from one burned house to another.
They now removing out of Canning Street (which
received goods in the morning) into Lombard
Street, and farther: and among others I now saw
my little goldsmith Stokes receiving some friend's
goods, whose house itself was burned the day after.
. . . . And I to Paul's Wharf, where I had appointed a boat to attend me, and took in Mr. Car-
casse and his brother, and carried them below and
above bridge too. And again to see the fire, which
was now got farther, both below and above, and no
likelihood of stopping it. Met the King and Duke
of York in their barge, and with them to Queen-
hith, and there called Sir Richard Browne to
them. Their order was only to pull down houses
apace, and so below bridge at the water side; but
little was, or could be done, the fire coming upon
them so fast. Good hopes there was of stopping it
the Three Cranes above, and at Buttolph's Wharf
below bridge, if care be used; but the wind carried
it into the City, so as we know not by the water side

what it do there. River full of lighters and boats
taking in goods, and good goods swimming in the
water, and only I observed that hardly one lighter
or boat in three that had the goods of a house in,
but there was a pair of virginals [spinets] in it.
Having seen as much as I could now, I away to
Whitehall by appointment, and there walked to
St. James's Park, and there met my wife, ...
and walked to my boat; and there upon the
water again, and to the fire up and down, it still
increasing, and the wind great. So near the fire
as we could for smoke ; and all over the Thames,
with one's faces in the wind, you were almost burned
with the shower of fire-drops. This is very true:
so as houses were burned by these drops and flakes
of fire, three or four, nay, five or six houses, one
from another. When we could endure no more
upon the water, we to a little ale-house on the
Bankside, over against the Three Cranes, and there
stayed till it was dark almost, and saw the fire
grow, and as it grew darker, appeared more and
more, and in corners and upon steeples, and between
churches and houses, as far as we could see up the
hill of the City, in a most horrid malicious bloody
flame, not like the fire flame of an ordinary fire. . . .
We stayed till, it being darkish, we saw the fire as
only one entire arch of fire from this to the other
side the bridge, and in a bow up the hill for an

arch of above a mile long: it made me weep to see it. The churches, houses, and all on fire, and flaming at once; and a horrid noise the flames made, and the cracking of houses at their ruin. So home with a sad heart, and there find everybody discoursing and lamenting the fire; and poor Tom Hater come with some few of his goods saved out of his house, which was burned upon Fish Street Hill. I invited him to lie at my house, and did receive his goods, but was deceived in his lying there, the news coming every moment of the growth of the fire; so we were forced to begin to pack up our own goods, and prepare for their removal; and did by moonshine .... carry much of my goods into the garden, and Mr. Hater and I did remove my money and iron chests into my cellar, as thinking that the safest place. And got my bags of gold into my office, ready to carry away, and my chief papers of accounts also there, and my tallies into a box by themselves. So great was our fear, as Sir W. Batten hath carts come out of the country to fetch away his goods to-night. We did put Mr. Hater, poor man, to bed a little; but he got but very little rest, so much noise being in my house, taking down of goods.

"3*d.* About four o'clock in the morning, my Lady Batten sent me a cart to carry away all my money, and plate, and best things, to Sir W.

Rider's at Bednall Green. Which I did, riding
myself in my night-gown, in the cart; and, Lord!
to see how the streets and highways are crowded
with people, running and riding, and getting of
carts at any rate to fetch away things. I find
Sir W. Rider tired with being called up all night,
and receiving things from several friends. His
house full of goods, and much of Sir W. Batten's
and Sir W. Pen's. I am eased at my heart to have
my treasure so well secured. Then home, and
with much ado to find a way, nor any sleep all this
night to me nor my poor wife. But then all this
day she and I, and all my people, laboring to get
away the rest of our things, and did get Mr. Tooker
to get me a lighter to take them in, and we did carry
them (myself some) over Tower Hill, which was
by this time full of people's goods, bringing their
goods thither; and down to the lighter, which lay
at the next quay, above the Tower Dock. And
here was my neighbor's wife, Mrs. ——, with her
pretty child, and some few of her things, which
I did willingly give way to be saved with mine, but
there was no passing with anything through the
postern, the crowd was so great. The Duke of
York come this day by the office, and spoke to us,
and did ride with his guard up and down the City
to keep all quiet (he being now General, and having the care of all). This day, Mercer being not

at home, but against her mistress' order gone to her
mother's and my wife going thither to speak with
W. Hewer, beat her there, and was angry. . . . .
At night lay down a little upon a quilt of W.
Hewer's in the office, all my own things being
packed up or gone ; and after me my poor wife
did the like, we having fed upon the remains of
yesterday's dinner, having no fire nor dishes, nor
any opportunity of dressing anything.

"*4th.* Up by break of day, to get away the rest
of my things ; which I did by a lighter at the Iron
Gate: and my hands so full, that it was the afternoon before we could get them all away. Sir W.
Pen and I to the Tower Street, and there met the
fire burning three or four doors beyond Mr. How-
ell's, whose goods, poor man, his trays, and dishes,
and shovels, etc., were flung all along Tower Street
in the kennels, and people working therewith from
one end to the other ; the fire coming on in that
narrow street, on both sides, with infinite fury. Sir
W. Batten not knowing how to remove his wine,
did dig a pit in the garden, and laid it there ; and
I took the opportunity of laying all the papers of
my office that I could not otherwise dispose of.
And in the evening Sir W. Pen and I did dig another, and put our wine in it ; and I my parmazan
cheese, as well as my wine and some other things.
. . . . This afternoon, sitting melancholy with

Sir W. Pen in our garden, and thinking of the certain burning of this office, without extraordinary means, I did propose for the sending up of all our workmen from the Woolwich and Deptford yards, ... and to write to Sir W. Coventry to have the Duke of York's permission to pull down houses, rather than lose this office, which would much hinder the King's business. So Sir W. Pen went down this night, in order to the sending them up to-morrow morning. . . . . Only now and then, walking into the garden, saw how horribly the sky looks, all on a fire in the night, was enough to put us out of our wits; and, indeed, it was extremely dreadful, for it looks just as if it was at us, and the whole heaven on fire. I after supper walked in the dark down to Tower Street, and there saw it all on fire, at the Trinity House on that side, and the Dolphin Tavern on this side, which was very near us; and the fire with extraordinary vehemence. Now begins the practice of blowing up of houses in Tower Street, those next the Tower, which at first did frighten people more than anything; but it stopped the fire where it was done, it bringing down the houses to the ground in the same places they stood, and then it was easy to quench what little fire was in it, though it kindled nothing almost. W. Hewer this day went to see how his mother did, and comes late home, telling us how he hath been forced to remove her to Islington, her house in Pye Corner being burned; so that the fire is got so far that way, and to the Old Bayly, and was running down to Fleet Street; and Paul's is burned, and all Cheapside. I wrote to my father to-night, but the post-office being burned, the letter could not go.

"*5th.* I lay down in the office again upon W. Hewer's quilt, mighty weary, and sore in my feet with going till I was hardly able to stand. About two in the morning my wife calls me up, and tells me of new cries of fire, it being come to Barking Church, which is at the bottom of our lane [Sethinge Lane]. I up; and finding it so, presently resolved to take her away, and did, and took my gold, which was about 2350*l.* W. Hewer and I are down by Proundy's boat to Woolwich; but, Lord! what a sad sight it was by moonlight to see the whole City almost on fire, that you might see it plain at Woolwich, as if you were by it. There, when I come, I find the gates shut, but no guard kept at all; which troubled me, because of discourses now begun, that there is a plot in it, and that the French had done it. I got the gates open, and to Mr. Shelden's, where I locked up my gold, and charged my wife and W. Hewer never to leave the room without one of them in it, night or day. . . . . Home, and whereas I expected **to**

have seen our house on fire, it being now about
seven o'clock; it was not. . . . . But going to
the fire, I find by the blowing up of houses, and the
great help given by the workmen out of the King's
yards, sent up by Sir W. Pen, there is a good stop
given to it, as well at Mark Lane end, as ours. . . . .
I up to the top of Barking steeple, and there saw
the saddest sight of desolation that I ever saw;
everywhere great fires, oil cellars, and brimstone,
and other things burning. I became afraid to stay
there long, and therefore down again as fast as I
could, the fire being spread as far as I could see it.
. . . . Received good hopes that the fire at our end is
stopped, they and I walked into the town, Fanchurch
Street, Gracious Street, and Lombard Street all in
dust. The Exchange a sad sight, nothing standing there but Sir Thomas Gresham's picture in the
corner. Into Moorfields (our feet ready to burn,
walking through the town among the hot coals),
and find that full of people, and poor wretches
carrying their goods there, and everybody keeping
his goods together by themselves. . . . . Drunk
there and paid twopence for a plain penny loaf.
Thence homeward, having passed through Cheapside, and Newgate Market, all burned; and seen
Antony Joyce's house in fire. . . . . And I
lay down and slept a good night about midnight.
. . . . But it is a strange thing to see how long

this time did look since Sunday, ... and I
had almost forgot the day of the week.

" 6*th*. Up about five o'clock ; . . . . and there
is now one broke out. . . . . I went with the
men, and we did put it out in a little time; so
that that was well again. It was pretty to see
how hard the women did work in the cannells
[street gutters] sweeping of water; but then
they would scold for drink, and be as drunk as
devils. . . . . And so to Westminster, thinking to
shift myself, being all in dirt from top to bottom;
but could not there find any place to buy a shirt
or a pair of gloves.

7*th*. Up by five o'clock; and, blessed be God,
find all well. . . . . My father's house, and the
Church, and a good part of the Temple the like.
So to Creed's lodging, near the New Exchange,
and there find him laid down upon a bed. . . . .
There borrowed a shirt of him, and washed . . . .
I home late to Sir W. Pen's. . . . . So here I
went the first time into a naked bed, only my
drawers on; and did sleep pretty well: but still
both sleeping and waking had a fear of fire in my
heart, that I took little rest."

I am sure that no intelligent person will read this
account of the fire by Pepys without pleasure and
profit. We follow him through the streets and on
the river; on the tower, and up the steeple. Every-

where he tells what he sees so simply that we see it also. We learn from these accounts of the fire that it is not safe to build cities of wood. Alas! how soon may the dreadful lesson again be taught by the destruction of some of our wooden cities. We see that the stone buildings in London suffered as much as did those of Chicago and Boston. We learn that brick was least liable to destruction by fire. We learn that if we build a city mostly of wood, even if the walls are of stone and brick, and omit to procure a proper defense from fire, that in the dry time and the great wind, a little fire neglected will soon become a dreadful disaster. And we also learn that, in the wonderful goodness and mercy of an Almighty Providence, an awful conflagration may become the greatest blessing to a city.

As but few people can now know what the plague really was, which was thus burned out of London, a few extracts from Maitland's history are inserted. It appeared in May of the year before the fire for the last time. More than sixty-eight thousand persons died of it, and ninety-seven thousand was the bill of mortality for the year 1665. The first week, when nine persons died, it created some alarm. It soon increased to forty-three. In June, the number was four hundred and seventy per week, and "it put the nobility, gentry, and principal citizens upon the wing of safety, all being instantly in an amazing hurry, and the city emptying itself into the country, the roads were excessively crowded with travellers and passengers." But in July, the bill increasing to two thousand and ten (per week), " all houses were shut up, the streets deserted, and scarce anything to be seen therein but grass growing, innumerable fires for purifying the infected air, coffins, pest-carts, red crosses upon doors, with the inscription, ' Lord, have mercy upon us ! ' and poor women in tears, with dismal aspects, and woeful lamentations, carrying their infants to the grave." And scarcely any other sounds to be heard than those incessantly emitted from the windows, of " Pray for us ! " and the dreadful call of " *Bring out your dead !* "

" In the month of September Death rode triumphant, for having (if I may be allowed the expression) borrowed Time's scythe, he mowed down the people like grass." The first week the burials were almost seven thousand ; the next, there were five hundred less ; but the week following, when the number was seven thousand one hundred and sixty-five, the people " fell into an abyss of horror and despair," " for now they fell into an apprehension that in a few days the living would not suffice to bury the dead." From this time it decreased, until the city was restored to its usual health.

Of the great plague of 1348 we read as follows: " The rejoicings which had spread over the whole nation for the conquest of Calais, and other great exploits and successes of King Edward in France, were soon damped, especially in this his capital city, where a terrible pestilence, that broke out in India, and in its western progress ravaged all the countries through which it passed in the most horrible manner, by sweeping away near all the inhabitants of each, and at length arriving in this city, carried off such a multitude of people, that it reduced provisions very low, as may be seen in the following specimen : —

" A fine horse, formerly worth 40*s.*, at 6*s.* 8*d.*

" The best fed ox at 4*s.* 0*d.* ; the best cow 1*s.* 0*d.* ; the best heifer or steer 0*s.* 6*d.*

" The best wether 0*s.* 4*d.* ; the best ewe 0*s.* 3*d.* ; the best lamb 0*s.* 2*d.* ; hog 0*s.* 5*d.*"

It continued to increase until the burial grounds could not contain the dead, and a lot was purchased by the Bishop of London, and more than 50,000 persons were buried there. And even this was not capacious enough, and others were built in which no less than 50,000, or 100,000 in all, were buried who died from this dreadful pestilence which " broke out in India." Did it not take the cholera roads ?

16

FIRES AT CONSTANTINOPLE.

This city has suffered more from dreadful fires than any other in the world in the last one hundred and fifty years.

In 1729, more than 12,000 buildings were destroyed, and 7,000 persons perished.

In 1745, a dreadful fire lasted eight days, of which we have no details.

In 1749, one fire burned 12,000, and another 10,000 buildings.

In 1751, 4,000 houses were burned.

In 1756, a fire burned 500, and another 15,000 buildings, and 100 persons.

There were great fires in 1761, 1765, 1767, 1769, and 1771.

In 1778, 2,000 buildings were destroyed.

In 1782, the first fire burned 600, the second 7,000, and the third 10,000 buildings, 50 Mosques and 100 corn mills.

In 1784, 10,000, and in 1791, 32,000 buildings were burned.

In 1792, and 1795, two fires burned 14,000 buildings.

Since that time a standing article of European news has been "Great Fire in Constantinople." Another has been one ridiculing the system of small engines used there.

In 1870, 7,000 houses were destroyed, and the loss was said to be $125,000,000. That the number of buildings and amount of loss is exaggerated while crossing the ocean, is to be hoped by every humane person, but the accounts, to those who know the amount of misery they must involve, seems shocking. Small engines only are used, and for a long time I was troubled to know how there were so many dreadful fires. At last I found the following account by a traveller. "For the citizens dare not quench the fires that burn their houses, because officers are appointed for that purpose." Oh, the millions of millions worth of property destroyed in other countries in that same manner.

But the manner of using those little engines. They are about as far apart as the steamers are in Boston, and get to work often in from fifteen to twenty minutes, when the fires have become so hot as to make it almost impossible to throw water from them upon the fires. The Boston Department could hardly do worse with them! But when a nation or a city continues for centuries to allow such buildings, and such a fire protective system, as shall make such awful results as have been recorded at Constantinople, is it not a duty of the nations in congress, to force them into common sense ideas, or to merge them into other nations, which will make them keep up in the onward march of the world?

There have been plenty of such national congresses in the interests of the rulers of Europe. Now let us have them in the interest of humanity.

THE QUEBEC CONFLAGRATION OF 1866.

The great conflagration at Quebec, October 1866, burned 2,500 buildings, rendered houseless 18,000 persons, and was one of the most disastrous of the many great and distressing fires which ever afflicted that city. The actual loss, $3,000,000, was much less than that of many fires in the United States, but the number of poor people who were thrown upon the world penniless, and with only the clothing on their persons, was probably greater than had ever occurred from any fire in the United States. And now for the lesson. " About five o'clock yesterday morning (Sunday), the flames were bursting out over Trudel's shop or bar-room in the lower flat. They were first discovered by the lower police, who at once raised the alarm, and their numbers being soon augmented by a few persons who chanced to be passing on their way to church, for their morning devotions, the door was burst in, and an attempt made to stifle the fire, but it proved ineffectual, as the opening of the doors only served to give vent to the flames, and before a few minutes had elapsed, the whole interior of the house, which was a wooden one, was in a blaze, the inmates having only time to save themselves." This idea of stifling the flames by bursting open the doors before there was water at hand with which to quench it, was one of great brilliancy, and should be remembered, so that we may avoid similar disasters ?

" By the time the alarm was given, and the Fire Brigade had arrived, the fire had made rapid headway, having communicated to the adjoining house on the west side, and was burning with great fury." A northeast gale was blowing at the time, and when the engines were ready to throw their streams of water upon the spreading flames, there was no water, *nor could they get a drop for more than an hour.*

A description of such a fire is needless. Other reasons than the want of water were given for the great magnitude of the conflagration; such as drunken gambling in the groggery all night, the crowded wooden buildings, etc., but they may be omitted.

When a fire occurs in the midst of a hundred acres of crowded wooden buildings, the wind blowing a gale at the time, and we are told that for more than an hour there was no water for the engines, we have no need to inquire for further reasons why the fire was not quenched until twenty-five hundred buildings were destroyed. But we do think that almost every "Yankee" will "guess," it would be best to have "two strings to one's bow;" either to have insured a supply of water, or to have prevented the fire from being "smothered by bursting open the doors" as long as possible!

THE CHICAGO FIRE.

Extracts from the report of the Chicago Fire and Police Commissioners on the great conflagration.

"The fire originated in a two-story barn in the rear of 137 De Koven Street. . . . . Intelligent citizens who lived near the fire testify that it was ten or fifteen minutes from the time they first saw the fire before any engines came upon the ground. . . . . When they arrived there were from three to five buildings fiercely burning. The fire must have been burning from ten to fifteen minutes, and with the wind blowing strongly from the southwest, and carrying the fire from building to building in a neighborhood composed wholly of dry wooden buildings, with wood shavings piled in every barn and under every house, the fire had got under too great headway for the engines called out by the first alarm to be able to subdue it. . . . . Upon arriving at the fire, Marshal Williams ordered the second, and soon after the third alarm to be turned in; but these only called the distant engines, and many valuable minutes elapsed before they could reach the fire and get to work, when the strong wind had scattered the fire into many buildings, all dry as tinder, spread it over so large an area the whole department were unable to cut it off or prevent the gale from carrying burning shingles and brands over their heads, and setting on fire buildings far away from the main fire. After it had got into the high church at the corner of Clinton and Mathew streets, and thence to the match factory and Bateman's planing mills and lumber, it was beyond the control of the fire department."

Extract from Chief Engineer Damrell's report, of the Boston Department.

" The great fire on Sunday night originated in a stable on De Koven Street. It was discovered by a policeman when it was very small. Hoping to extinguish it without sounding an alarm, he set to work to do so, but finding the fire was too much for him, he called," etc.

So we see that the fire, when first seen, was very small. There is no doubt in the minds of those who know the power of small engines, that one or two of them would have kept the fire in the first building, and a few would have put out easily every fire which caught on the three or four buildings from it. And all this before the arrival of the hose carriage, eleven, or the engines, nine and six blocks away. So the fire, having nothing to arrest it, until the opposing force was as nothing, cut a rather narrow swath of flame through

the city. " Why," said a sufferer, " when the fire
caught upon that house," pointing to a new house,
" two houses three or four blocks off, over where
you see those double houses, were all on fire." An
owner of a planing mill said: " The fire had
passed by, and we thought we were safe, when all
at once the fire was all around us." Nothing will
so well describe how this happened as to repeat the
old saying, describing a storm of snow and wind
— "round and round the house and peeps in every
crack." Just that happened after the fire had
cut the first swath of its awful night's work, and
the engines had left to keep it if possible, somewhere in check. The cart-loads of living coals
flew on the wings of the wind into every crack and
cranny, under, over, and upon every building to
the right of the track of the fire, when, of course,
there being no protection against them, some of
them were soon in flames. Instantly the first
scene was acted over; a new swath went flying
after the first, and then another, until, as we were
told by an intelligent person, " the fire went rushing down four or five times, one after another,
right through the city." This was one of the
ways that the fire seemed, as has been said, to
"back up against the wind." So the little one,
which could have been crushed out in a few minutes (see the " Chicago Tribune " of December

13) became a thousand, and one hundred and sixty acres of the West Division of Chicago in a few hours was a smoking, blackened mass of ruins. When the fire reached the great buildings, the tremendous heat, excited by the force of the gale, set fire to the right of the line of fire faster than the coals, and they found no mischief to do. The force opposing the fire was steam fire-engines, and not half enough of them. That the men did their duty I have not a doubt, but the system is just what batteries were in our late war, splendid when supported by infantry, but unsupported, just what the engines were at Chicago. Not one victory should we have won against an army armed with batteries and infantry, with only batteries for our brave defenders. So we see defeat after defeat in our battles with the element of fire, great fires here, there, and everywhere ; and so we shall continue to do until we adopt the common-sense system in our fire department which is now established throughout the armies of the civilized world.

THE BOSTON FIRE.

This great conflagration, which destroyed seven hundred and seventy-six buildings, and an immense amount of other property, valued in all at $80,000,000, commenced in a building numbered

83 and 85 Summer Street. When first seen, the
fire was in the basement. With the new *fire preventive* system described in this work, it would
probably have been extinguished there, and without an alarm to the city. But no such common-
sense system had been adopted, and although
thousands of people soon arrived at the spot, the
flames, first doubling, and then quadrupling every
minute, leaped up the elevators, and a roaring,
raging fire was set in every loft, and in the roof.
No one of them gave the alarm to the firemen
until it had been seen in the city of Charlestown
and the towns of Belmont and Watertown, and
no doubt in many other towns in the vicinity of
Boston.   Fifteen minutes after the Charlestown
police saw it, — a great fire on the first building, —
and at least five minutes after, two men drove from
the Payson estate, in Belmont, where they saw the
fire burst out into a great flame, which they supposed was not a mile away, to the Mount Auburn
post-office, where they found the alarm had been
given, and the fire found to be too distant to take
small engines, the Boston Fire Department had not
been notified that there was a fire in Boston.
For this strange neglect, precisely the same which
caused the destruction of Chicago, neither the
Boston department nor the telegraph were to
blame.   The people of Boston collected by thou-

sands to see a great fire, but every one of them neglected to do what would have saved a great number of lives and nearly $80,000,000. If any person not employed in or owning a building on fire was paid five dollars for doing this service only when there was a fire, all that dreadful fire would have been prevented. But this is not all. "Too much is left to the firemen, and we do too little to protect ourselves," say the English works on this subject. The foolish, senseless saying, "I never go to a fire until the walls are so hot that I cannot lay in bed," has lost many a house, store, warehouse, shop, etc. Every man, aye, every woman, should, when a fire is in their immediate neighborhood, at once see if they cannot help to extinguish it, and go away only when they cannot be of service, or the firemen arrive and want their places. But the devil has checkmated this good intent also. I have known a man in Cambridge run with a little engine on his arm to fires, and get so instantly to work that the fires would often be all out before the great engines could be got to work. And I have known the great engine's stream, when the fire was out, and the people of the house were thanking him for saving their home, thrown full in his face for putting out the fire. No, the people feel that the firemen must, and they must not, put out a fire.

A most unfortunate state of things was seen when the telegraph did give the alarm. The danger that the heat from the first building would set fire to those opposite and on the side of it, increased every minute; yet the engines came slowly to their work, and then could not throw water upon the roofs of the exposed buildings, where was the greatest danger.

It was just here that the fire department failed, and allowed the fire to become a conflagration. There were rows of wooden tarred paper roofs upon which once catching hold, the fire could run like a race-horse in half a dozen different directions; but a little stream thrown back on the Mansard roofs of the exposed buildings would have protected them. Alas! the steamers failed; it was a one idea department; no other method had been thought of in Boston, though used for years in Paris and London. The fire caught, and ran its horrible race through and over the doomed city. But think of that Mansard roof on Otis Street, which, catching fire, was the cause of the dire disaster. It is not on fire now, though the heat is tremendous, and it must soon be in flames, unless water can be thrown upon it. The steamers cannot do it, and there is no other means at the hands of the Boston Fire Department. But a small engine, throwing no more than six gallons of water per minute from the inside, out, and back upon the exposed roof, would have made it as impossible to take fire as if it had been thrown by an earthquake into the Atlantic Ocean! Other little engines would have kept the fire from the stores on the sides, and there would have been a loss of only one building and its contents. Instead of horrid rivers of fire, running in half a dozen directions, roaring, crashing, flashing, devouring streets and squares, with the steamers and their men from all New England working in vain, there would have been seen a little stream held by an arm covered with wet cloths, and the loss would have been $100,000 instead of $80,000,000!

Do not laugh at this, unless you have done your best to save buildings in similar places and failed. Even then, do not be too sure, for another might succeed when you did not. The Quincy fireman, out on the roof at Hovey's store, saved that without even an engine, but with great danger to his life; and if that had been lost, so would have been the store. I know of that which I write. I have been successful when a wooden building was in the most imminent danger of bursting into flame from the heat of a great fire opposite. I have thrown a little stream of water from the upper window, which, cooling the top of the building as the nurse does the face, hands, etc., of the raging, fevered patient, it trickled down to the bottom, doing the same blessed work in its downward progress. As the fire opposite grew more furious, the glass cracked like frost-work, and the white window-curtains toasted brown through the glass. But the hand and arm, enveloped in a wet shawl, held the little pipe, and the water, never failing,—though half a dozen men fainted in the room, almost a furnace,—kept on its steady work of bathing the outside of the building. It stands now at Brighton; and with the same apparently tiny means at the Boston fire, the store which took fire from the first would now be standing, and seven hundred and seventy-four other buildings, and seventy-nine millions of dollars which were destroyed would have been saved!

The one idea system of only a few great steam fire-engines, which go splurging through the streets, and which, though wonderfully efficient in many places after they have got to work, for fighting fires, can be of no more use for preventing others, than would be a six hundred pounder for killing mosquitoes, or a three-inch revolver for penetrating the walls of a ten inch plated iron-clad, should be abandoned. We may double, triple, or quadruple our steam fire-engines, and double their power; we may add great, monstrous

" extinguishers," drawn by powerful horses; we may adopt all the wonderful so-called improvements which have been advertised in the papers since the fire, at an expense of millions of dollars, but the whole city of Boston will not be one tenth part as well protected as it will by the four thousand small engines, as described in this work, at a less expense the first year than the introduction of one steam fire-engine.

Examine the weapons of an army, — great guns, for the reduction of forts and batteries, muskets, rifles, and revolvers; of the navy, six hundred pounders, and from those down to muskets, rifles, and revolvers. Look at our means of travel — from the great train of cars to the dog-cart and shanks-mare ; our business teams — from the lumbering six horse or ox wagon to the pretty express drawn by a pony; at our fish-hooks — from the great hook for catching sharks to the one half an inch long for catching smelts. If a physician wishes to give an injection, does he use for the purpose a steam fire or a manual engine ? or if a child has the croup, and he wishes to give it ipecac, does he give it half a dozen pounds or so ? or to bleed a patient, does he cut off the jugular vein ? If a farmer wishes to plough his land, from which he has just taken off a hundred cords of wood per acre, and which is full of stumps, rocks, and roots, would he use a little one horse plough? or if he used a great, heavy plough on the rough piece, and it did the work well, would he use that to work up his garden beds? If he came home hungry, would he refuse to eat his dinner because he could not swallow it at one gulp, or because his wife placed by his plate a knife and fork instead of a manure fork and shovel? We understand all this; but when we come to the question of extinguishing fires, which of all others vary most in size, we simply use means of one size, and then make such an arrangement that it will not be possible for an attack to be made in less than fifteen minutes, while the fire goes on increasing, at first doubling, and soon quadrupling every minute! Who can wonder that the "Fire Record" of the daily papers is so large, or that there are so many great fires and conflagrations, or towns and cities destroyed. And the fires will go on increasing in number (it will not be easy to go beyond that of Chicago) until we apply the same common-sense rules for building and at fires which we do at our common avocations.

May a merciful Providence direct us to be wise in time to avert another such dreadful disaster as we have just passed through. I am aware that I am telling the tale of small engines over and over again; but if I am correct in my statements, it cannot be told too many times — that is, until the engines are introduced throughout the country, and the fires cease to be dangerous, when I will cease to talk or write of them.

THE FIRE AT CHICOPEE.

" One of our best workmen was in the wheel-room at work. He had a shop-lantern of the best kind, filled with sperm oil. By an accidental blow this lantern was broken, igniting the grease and lint on and under the gearing, which was at no time in motion. From this point the flames flashed over the accumulated lint on the belts, and in the belt passages from floor to floor. So rapid was the spread of the fire, that the mechanic, together with the watchman who immediately arrived, could only remain long enough to throw two or three pails of water upon it, which seemed to increase rather than diminish its force. They then obtained water from the adjoining rooms and the canal, but found their efforts unavailing, and immediately gave a general alarm. The pump-room being on fire the pumps could not be started.

" J. W. Osgood, *Agent*."

The workman was one of the best, and so was the lantern, and so was the oil. Therefore no one

17

was to blame.   The mills must be burned, and the loss, $900,000, be borne as it best can by the insurance companies and the stockholders.   If they are satisfied, — and the agent says, " the insurance inspectors are, and that they absolve us from all blame, and feel that everything was done to save the property," — who shall complain, who shall dare to find fault ?   That is one side of the picture. Let us look at another side of it.   It is a fact then that the wheel-room of these great cotton factories may contain, and some do, so much grease and lint that if once on fire, it may, in spite of any preventive force, flash up from story to story, so that in a few minutes the whole building will be in flames.   Now suppose that it was necessary that the work was to be done at ten o'clock, A. M., instead of ten o'clock, P. M.   What would have been the result ?   Why, that two or three hundred or more working girls and men would have been roasted alive !   In the name of humanity I protest against this horrid danger, not of cruelty to animals, but to the poor workwomen who are lured into such dangerous places for a pittance of a dollar more or less per day.   How many other wheel-rooms in Massachusetts, in New England, in the United States, are all ready with the lint and grease, to, at the slightest, and most proper and respectable accident, repeat the horror of the fire in the Church of Santiago, Chili, by burning all their inmates? Is there no remedy? If not, let us know it, so that the poor women may earn their daily bread at some more safe avocation.

But there is another view. How much grease is required in the wheel-room? The great cog-wheels, which, turning, put in motion all the machinery, must be continually oiled. For this purpose in this mill an amount filling a tank four or five feet in diameter and from fifteen to eighteen inches deep, was in constant use. More than a barrel of this inflammable mixture mixed with the lint, and surrounded by the dry lint, so that at any accident it might fly from story to story almost instantly setting fire to the whole building! How many such fires have there been? How many more will there be? How soon will hundreds of poor creatures perish in such a fire? Now for the remedy. Such tanks must no longer be used. Another kind are made and in use at Lowell, and no doubt at other places, of cast-iron, and in such a way that it perhaps is impossible for their contents to take fire. Again, the lint must not be allowed to gather until it may become dangerous if on fire. Do the agents say they cannot do it? Then shut down your mills. That will clean off the lint in an hour! And once more, pails of water. Mr. Braidwood has recommended pumps to put out just such fires in the London warehouses, and Mr. John L. Hays tells of their great efficiency in mills. For putting out the fire in the tank, I have no doubt an extinguisher would have been an efficient machine ; for dashing out the lint on the walls, the small pumps would have been the best. Again, one workman should not go alone into such a place to work. Another man, with a pump to dash out in a moment a fire, as is done in the theatres at Paris, would have prevented all the fire and loss. In London, one man alone is never allowed in a house on fire. The tank of grease could have been covered at very little expense.

The "grease" is made safe in some factories, and the lint of course can be. For the protection of the lives of the inmates, for the interest of the stockholders and the insurance companies, and for the general safety of cities, should not there be a person in the interest of the State whose duty it would be to have charge of such important interests as the safety of these great buildings from fire ?

NEW YORK'S DANGER.

That every man, horse, engine, and all the other appliances of the Fire Department of New York are as nearly perfect as possible, I do not presume to doubt; but the city, from the vicinity of Trinity Church to beyond Union Square, is constructed in such a manner that should a fire occur in a dry time, and in a gale of wind, it might end in a conflagration to which those of Boston and Chicago would seem only as bonfires.

The Holly system, perhaps the best in the world, invented by Mr. Holly of Lockport, New York, should be adopted, and Mr. Holly instructed to place in the portion indicated, the very best and most powerful engines he can construct (in the smallest possible time). They should be kept in full working force in every high wind. These, with his new hydrants containing hose, to be placed near the doors of warehouses and manufactories, by which great streams could be thrown almost instantly upon fires, and the hydrants in the streets, would be equal to many hundreds of steam fire-engines. New York has expended millions for its parks and squares; now let it give one or two millions to prevent its destruction by fire.

CHAPTER XI.

CONCLUSION.

THE following letter is selected from the work entitled " The Early Years of his Royal Highness the Prince Consort.   Compiled under the direction of the Queen."

" COBURG, 18*th October*, 1838.

" DEAR GRANDMAMMA, — I have again delayed writing to you, but when a man is once sunk in idleness, it is difficult to get out of it.

" I learned from your dear letter to Ernest, that you are better, and that you have moved into your pretty winter residence, in all its new splendor.

" How perishable it all is, we felt seriously yesterday, when, if God had not held his protecting hand over us, the whole palace of Coburg might have become a prey to the flames, nor we ourselves able in any way to escape.

" A fire is lit in our rooms every morning, lest we should find them cold when we come down to town occasionally in the afternoon.

" It happened the day before yesterday, that we stayed in town after the play, in order not to catch cold driving back to the Rosenarr. The next morning I was awakened by an unpleasant smell. I sprang out of bed to see whether the register had not been forgotten to be opened in one of the stoves. The smoke met me thicker and thicker, but I could not discover anything. In the fourth room I was met by the flames darting towards me ; it was all on fire. I called out fire ! fire ! when Ernest and Cart came from their rooms to my assistance. No living soul was in this wing of the palace, except us three ; it was also so early that nobody was astir in the neighborhood. You can fancy our alarm. We did not take long to consider, but closed all the doors and shut ourselves up with the fire. There were only two jugs of water and one with camomile tea at our command, of which we made the most. Ernest took my cloak and his own and threw them upon the flames, while I dragged all my bedding there and pressed the mattresses and large counterpanes against the burning wall. Cart (their servant) lifted a marble table with incredible strength, and threw it against a book-case enveloped in flames, causing it to fall down. Having thus subdued the fire, we could think of calling for more help.

"Ernest ran, just as he got out of bed, downstairs to the sentry, who gave the alarm, while I and Cart were still working up-stairs. The heat and smoke were so powerful that all the windows had fallen out; even the glasses of the framed pictures were cracked, and the pictures shriveled. in, and the paint of the doors is quite charred.

"Help now came in haste from all sides; a number of workmen brought water up and extinguished the smouldering fire. A book-stand with many books, and all our prints, two chairs and a table, a looking-glass, etc.; have been burnt.

" There is no other harm done but that Cart and I have burnt the soles of our feet, as we got barefooted into the cinders.

" The accident was caused by the ignorance of a stoker who had heated a stove that was not meant to be used, and on which books and prints were lying and against which a quantity of maps were standing. The only picture that was not injured is the one of the fire at the palace of Gotha. ·

" Farewell, now, dear Grandmamma, and always love your faithful grandson, ALBERT."

It is to be hoped that all the young ladies and gentlemen of America who imitate foreign people, may, if a fire occurs in their dwellings or in the immediate neighborhood, imitate those splendid firemen, Albert, afterwards the first gentleman of England, his brother and their servant Cart. A better fought fire, a better description of one, or a better letter to a grandmother, it will be difficult to find. Fires would be few and far between with such firemen. Think what they would have done with a small engine! I wish they had told us which was the best to extinguish fire, water or camomile tea. But the whole description is capital. There cannot be a doubt that those young gentlemen saved the splendid palace from destruction.

Among many descriptions of fire which I have, I select the following as one of the best lessons. An old lady hearing screams of distress from children, caught a blanket and ran into the room from whence came the cries, to find that the clothes of her two grandchildren of eight and ten years of age were on fire. One of them had gone too near the open fire, and her clothes catching fire the clothes of the other caught, while she was trying to help her sister. Throwing them down instantly, she pressed the blanket upon them, smothering out the blaze, and then as quickly as possible she extinguished the rest of the fire. The children were dreadfully burned, as were the hands of the grandmother, but the fire had reached no vital part before they were thrown down, and they were soon well and in that class of children who are careful of fire, as it is to be hoped all children will be.

GREAT TRIUMPH OF THE BOSTON FIRE DEPART-
MENT.

BOSTON, *July* 7, 1876.

The people of Boston passed last night through
a trial of intense excitement and danger, and
thanks to the splendid working of the new fire
department, the city has been preserved from
destruction.   Our new department has been the
scene of no little rivalry for the past few months,
and while the small engines of course have put out
four out of five fires, the steamers have dashed and
smashed out several which in ordinary times would
have resulted in great fires or conflagrations.   Last
night the wind from the southwest was truly terrific.   At about twelve o'clock an immense structure at the south part of the city used as a wood
planing-mill, and for workers of wood generally,
was found to be on fire.   Before the telegraph
gave an alarm the fire had flown up the old fash-
ioned elevator, and the hatchway for letting chips
etc., to the basement, into every one of the six
stories, and the windows being open, before an
engine large or small got to work, there was a
mass of fire two hundred feet square and eighty
feet high, roaring and crashing before the spectators, while great pieces of wood flew from the roof
upon other buildings.   The excitement of those

looking on became intense. The wooden signs, and the windows of all the buildings opposite were soon smoking, or in flames, and no help seemed likely to prevent the destruction of the city. But in an incredibly short space of time, one window and another opened on each of the four sides of the great fiery furnace, and little pipes were held out by arms covered with wet woolen cloths, and the outsides of all the buildings were kept wet and cool with water. The immense amount of steam which rose where it was applied, told only too plainly of the great danger. Soon from one, and then another window, came great streams from the steamers which were thrown over into the burning building. In half an hour, no less than twenty such great streams were thrown across, which soon deadened the fire in the lower stories. By this time, however, the three upper stories and the Mansard roof, were one great raging, awful fire. Thousands of great flaming pieces of wood flew away, some a mile from the fire, crushing in windows, and setting fire in hundreds of places, while lesser pieces and millions of sparks flew over the entire length of the city, setting fires in every street, lane, and court, and even several in Charlestown, the Navy-yard, and Chelsea, while a small barn was burned away off at Revere. And now every person learned the wonderful efficiency of the small engines.   More than two thousand of them were on duty.   Not a fire could light on a building, but a stream was upon it in a minute. In one place, a fire·was not discovered until it had become so large as to seem quite beyond the control of the little pumps.   A panic was likely to ensue.   Screams and shrieks were the order of the moment, when a man with a pump came up and asking for water, took a pail to it, and soon the water was doing its blessed work.   He had not got rid of one pail before the fire was attacked on two other sides, and in three minutes the firemen were off for other fires.   Little fires were put out in every direction.   A spark, or small piece of wood, would light on a building, and the wind would force it into a blaze in a moment.   The next moment it would be dashed out.   The chief of the second brigade reports already eight hundred and seventy-four fires put out by them.   The people soon understood the danger, and the remedy, and water in pails and tubs was before almost every house on the line of the fire.   Never had the people of Boston such cause for thanksgiving, as on this the seventh of July, 1876.

P. S. — We are informed by the owners of the building destroyed, that they shall rebuild of a new material indestructible by fire.

In one of Dickens's works two men were said to be employed by the English government, whose duty it was to show " how not to do it." If any people wish " not to do " the work I have advocated in this book let them apply to the heads of the fire departments. But when you have proved that large and small engines combined are as practical and as useful as large and small arms in an army, go to work as did the press and the people in the late small-pox excitement; or as did the Hon. Samuel A. Elliot, who introduced the " paid fire department; " or later, as did the noble men who forced the present popular and excellent steam fire-engines into the Boston Fire Department. I know a gentleman of Boston whose wife once clung to him in an agony of fear and entreated him to give up the steam fire-engines, as she feared that if he persisted his life would be the forfeit. All the persons I have named, as do others, who have earnestly advocated any reform, however good and useful, know that there are " klu-klux " north, as well as south, of Mason and Dixon's line.

I have, in this book, endeavored to show how fires may be prevented. I have simply done what is the duty of every one who sees a fire, — given the alarm, as they would call " Fire." I have had many discouragements, family afflictions, a long-continued and painful malady, and a continual sense of my inability to do full justice to so important a question. But the subject is of such vast importance; fires are increasing so rapidly; that I have felt I had no right to hold my peace.

If the reforms I have endeavored to prove would be useful, by building almost entirely without wood, for dwelling-houses, and less high and really fire-proof stores and warehouses, and a preventive system by which fires may be instantly attacked, is not adopted, fires will continue to increase until the destruction of villages, towns, and cities will be so great as to involve the country in a great financial ruin.

I know how much more popular it would be to advocate the introduction of larger engines, and to appeal in that way to the popular feeling of the times. But I also know that would be but the means of keeping still longer the present popular but unsafe and inefficient system. The question is one of too much solemnity for equivocation. The truth must be told and the systems changed, or disasters like those of Portland, Chicago, and Boston will constantly fall upon us.

The awful loss of life and property, and the distress of thousands, aye, of hundreds of thousands of families from this cause, I think, make the following quotation from " Elijah " a proper conclusion of a book which seeks to prevent the present loss of life by clothing taking fire; to urge people to construct their dwellings of materials which fire cannot consume, and to induce them to adopt fire systems which will render impossible such dreadful conflagrations as have lately astonished the civilized world.

" Behold, God, the Lord, passed by; and a mighty wind rent the mountains around: brake in pieces the rocks; brake them before the Lord. But yet the Lord was not in the tempest. Behold, God, the Lord, passed by; and the sea was upheaved; and the earth was shaken. But yet the Lord was not in the earthquake. And after the earthquake there came a fire. But yet the Lord was not in the fire. And after the fire there came a still, small voice. AND IN THAT STILL, SMALL VOICE, ONWARD CAME THE LORD."

INDEX.

18

www.ingramcontent.com/pod-product-compliance
Lightning Source LLC
Chambersburg PA
CBHW030341270326
41926CB00009B/917